THE ONE WHO SAW VISIONS

THREE FRENCH SAINTS
THE ONE WHO SAW VISIONS

Bernadette Soubirous
(1844-1879)

Críostóir Ó Floinn

the columba press

First published in 2009 by
the columba press
55A Spruce Avenue, Stillorgan Industrial Park,
Blackrock, Co Dublin

Cover by Bill Bolger
Origination by The Columba Press
Printed in Ireland by ColourBooks Ltd, Dublin

ISBN 978-1-85607-659-3

Table of Contents

CHAPTER ONE

The Miller's Daughter

Bernadette Soubirous was born on 7 January 1844 in the small town of Lourdes which nestles below the Pyrenees mountain range dividing France from Spain. At the time of her birth, the population of Lourdes was just over 4,000; today, the resident population is nearly 20,000, but any visitor trying to make a way through the narrow streets crowded with pilgrims from all over the world would be justified in estimating the actual population at any one time as nearly a million. In France, only Paris has more hotels than modern Lourdes, and every street seems to consist of rows of cafés alternating with shops selling religious souvenirs and statues catering for all tastes and pockets.

While it is not necessary for an understanding of the story of what happened to the fourteen-year-old Bernadette on a day in February 1858 and subsequently, it us always of benefit to learn something of the actual locale and period of any event or story. Even a novel like *Pride and Prejudice* will be better understood and enjoyed if the reader first tries to imagine the circumstances and period in which Jane Austen, a single, well-educated woman of middle class status, with family connections to the British Navy, sat down with paper and pen in the corner of a quiet room and commenced her novel which would be published in 1813, two years before Waterloo.

Mention of Waterloo also helps to envisage the society into which Bernadette Soubirous was born in 1844. It was just over half a century since the upheaval and horrors of the French Revolution in 1789, it was only twenty-nine years after that final defeat of Napoleon Bonaparte in 1815, and twenty-three since his death in exile on St Helena. Most likely, then, as in every other town and village in France, there would have been, in Lourdes and its environs, veterans of varying ages, some of them probably minus a limb or bearing other scars of battle, telling winter tales at the firesides or in the cafés about the glories and horrors of war, perhaps even about that ignominious retreat from Moscow. As in the case of Jane Austen, we must eliminate from the world of Bernadette all such things as electricity, cars, planes, radio, television, phones, etc.

From the municipal archives of Lourdes we learn that when Bernadette was growing up in Lourdes the town had its own civic courts, 459 houses and 4,155 inhabitants. It had the usual markets and fairs of such a town, but over one thousand men worked in its slate and marble quarries. The town also had 7 innkeepers, 2 head waiters, 8 cooks, one roast-meat seller, 13 tavern-keepers, 6 soft-drink sellers, 18 wholesale merchants and traders, 2 hairdressers, 3 wig-makers, 120 professional people among whom were some judges and lawyers, two physicians, a chemist, a superindent of police and 7 constables.

The town also had a printing press, a newspaper, and a club, the haunt of the local intellectuals who, like similar types throughout France, were still strongly influenced in their thinking and attitudes by the brilliant anti-clericals of the previous century, Voltaire, Rousseau and others. The professional class, including the local clergy, would have been educated through the medium of standard French, and spoke that language, whereas the common people were generally illiterate and – an important point to note – spoke a dialect or *patois* that had its own vocabulary and expressions. The surrounding hills were pastureland for sheep, and many small mills were kept going by the strong streams rushing down to the Gave river far below the town. Over a short space on the Lapaca stream there were five such mills, and it was in one of these, the Boly mill, on 7 January 1844, that Bernadette was born, the first child of the miller, François Soubirous, and his young wife, Louise.

It was as a result of a tragic accident to another man that François Soubirous graduated from being a mere labourer in another local mill to become tenant of the Boly mill. On 1 July 1841, the miller of Boly, Justin Castérot, was killed when his cart over-turned on a road near Lourdes. His widow, Claire, was left not only with a family of four teenage daughters and two younger children – her own aged mother was also living with them – but also with the appalling discovery that her dead husband had not been the proprietor of the mill, as he thought, but merely a ten-ant paying an annual fee to the real owner. As there was no son old enough to take over, it was imperative that a capable man be found at once to keep the mill-wheel turning and the family from starvation.

The widow decided to try to make a match for her eldest daughter, Barnarde, aged 19. She settled on François Soubirous, a placid 34-year-old bachelor of good reputation who worked in the Latour mill. He responded to her invitation to visit, but the widow's plan ran into an unforeseen problem. Although custom decreed that daughters should be married off in order of age – the eldest child, male or female, held the position of heir and was second in authority to the parents – it became apparent, after the quiet man had made some visits to the household at the Casterot mill, that something was worrying him. He finally re-vealed to the anxious widow that he was ready and willing to marry her daughter – but not the one she proposed. He risked the fury and perpetual opposition of the eldest daughter by re-vealing that he fancied her blonde and blue-eyed younger sister, Louise, aged 17, and would marry her or be seen no more at the Boly mill. To the perturbed mother, he offered the diplomatic but lame excuse that he felt Louise would be a better housekeeper. Claire Casterot had no alternative but to accept the new match, hoping that the personal and social snub to Bernarde, the eldest of her daughters and the 'heir', would not be a cause of trouble until such time as another marriage solved the problem.

Thus it was that François Soubirous became tenant of the Boly mill, the husband of 17-year-old Louise Casterot and, a year later, on 7 January 1844, the father of a girl who was des-tined to achieve as much fame as Napoleon Bonaparte himself,

THE ONE WHO SAW VISIONS

albeit in a somewhat different area of human affairs. Fortunately for all concerned, the eldest girl, Bernarde, accepted the situation with good grace, helped by retaining her authoritative position as 'heir' and by the fact that Louise, a gentle and patient girl, felt embarrassed rather than triumphant at the way things had turned out. Bernarde became a loving godmother to the first child of her younger sister, and in testimony many years later would say proudly of the baby, Bernadette, 'She knew me as well as she knew her mother.' The time would come when Bernadette, aged 12, would go to work as a servant in a house and café owned by her Aunt Bernarde in order to lessen the number of mouths to be fed in her own poverty-stricken family; but until her death at the age of 35, the contrasting sounds of her childhood, the gushing mill stream and the harsh grinding of the millstone, would echo in her memory.

CHAPTER TWO

Life at the Mill

By the standards of the labouring class of society into which she had been born, life for the child Bernadettte, living as she did in one of the many small mills of Lourdes and similar Pyrenean towns, was a hand-to-mouth existence not securely above the level of poverty. In ancient times, after someone first made bread from flour, the production of the daily bread involved severe manual labour. In the *Odyssey*, composed about 700 BC, Homer incidentally reveals the literal slavery involved in this process in an outhouse of the palace of Odysseus 'where the millstones for grinding the king's corn were kept, and where twelve women laboured together, grinding the barley and wheat that nourish people. The other women were gone to their sleep by now, having ground their load of corn; only the one who was the weakest of them was not yet finished.' Odysseus overhears the plaintive cry of this poor slavewoman when she stopped her handmill for a moment and prayed to Zeus to be delivered 'from the terrible drudgery of this grinding that has worn my poor knees away'.

Before mechanisation, human genius found ways of using animals or the forces of nature to eliminate that 'terrible drudgery' of the handmill. Windmills and watermills became a feature of the landscape, and the new occupation of miller was an added factor in the local community. Cervantes made a famous literary incident out of his crazy hero, the would-be knight errant, Don Quijote de la Mancha, charging windmills mistaken for giants. Even when I was growing up in Limerick there were areas still called 'the Windmill' and 'the Mill road', with no mill in sight, although at the end of the Mill road, beside the River

Shannon, some long-dead miller had left us an outdoor swim-
ming pool still known as the Mill stream; in that invigorating,
fast-flowing channel children learned to swim long before the
advent of chlorinated indoor pools.

Because of the number of small mills in an area like Lourdes,
the occupation of miller did not guarantee a constant supply of
the daily bread even for the table of the miller himself. Two factors would affect the profitability of mills like the Boly mill in
which Bernadette was born: the vagaries of weather affected the
quality and quantity of the corn available from the surrounding
countryside, while the industry of the individual miller, and his
business acumen in ensuring a sufficient supply of grain, whatever its seasonal quality, was the crucial element in the success
or failure of the business.

By all accounts, Bernadette's father was neither lazy nor in-
competent, but he was lacking in that pragmatic dedication to
the detail of business which distinguishes the realistic grafter
from the well-intentioned but misplaced practitioner in the
sphere of commerce. He also had the handicap of being strictly
honest and morally upright in his business, unlike that boisterous and lascivious miller who was one of the diverse group encountered by the English poet, Geoffrey Chaucer (1340-1400) on
the pilgrimage to the shrine of St Thomas à Becket at
Canterbury. Of that rogue the poet says, in *The Canterbury Tales*,

Wel coude he stelen corn and tollen thryes,
And yet he had a thombe of gold, pardee.

The metaphorical 'thumb of gold' was used in falsely judg-
ing the quality of the farmers' grain, thus ensuring the three-fold
profit, 'tollen thryes'.

When he married into the Boly mill, the staid and steady
François Soubirous found himself in a situation that added further problems to those common to his profession. His mother-
in-law, the widowed Claire Casterot, was still in residence along
with her family – from her grandmother to her youngest aunt,
aged four, the new baby, Bernadette, had five women to pet her

– and although some of the older girls probably went out to do casual work, the mill was the source of sustenance for many more mouths than those of the miller and his young wife. That same young wife, depicted unanimously in all later evidence as a loving, gentle and patient mother and wife, was to prove a liability insofar as the commercial viability of the mill was concerned. Apparently, her kind heart and good nature caused her not only to offer hospitality to customers and casual visitors, including beggars, but also to allow credit to those who did not have ready cash for the flour and other foodstuffs of which they were in immediate and desperate need. Consequently, the Boly mill became attractive to those customers whose conscience is of the same elastic quality as the credit they seek from such sources as the naïve and soft-hearted young woman at the Boly mill.

The combination of factors militating against commercial success at the Boly mill would inevitably grind out misfortune for its inhabitants as surely as the millstone itself ground the wheat from the mill's suppliers; but that trouble was still not even a cloud on the horizon when Bernadette was born. However, trouble in another form struck while she was still a ten-month-old babe in arms. One winter everning in 1844, Bernadette's mother, Louise, now expecting her second child, was drowsing in a chair by the fire when a resin candle hanging from the chimney fell on her. She suffered severe injuries, including burns to her breasts that ruled out any further sustenance from them. That Bernadette at the age of ten months was still dependant on her mother's breast-milk for nourishment will surprise only those who believe that new-born babies should be fed from the same source as calves. The poor have always been glad to delay adding another share to the division of whatever food can be put on the table, and an extended period of breast-feeding was considered to be effective in that regard. Anyone who has read *An tOileánach*, an account of life in the Great Blasket Island off the coast of Kerry by Tomás Ó Criomhthain (1856-1937), translated into English by Robin Flower, will recall that, although he was, as he says in the original, *'dríodar an chrúiscín, deireadh an áil'* (the lees of the jug, the last of the brood) Tomás claims to remember being at his mother's breast and to have been four years old before he was 'taken from suckling'.

Bernadette's Aunt Bernarde, her young mother's older sister, went looking for a wet-nurse for her beloved godchild. She found one in the hilly district of Bartrès about four kilometres from Lourdes. Marie Laguës, wife of a clog-maker, had just suffered the loss of her first-born child, a son, only eighteen days old. She agreed to nurse Bernadette for a payment of five francs a month, payable in grain or silver. Although Bernadette was weaned by December 1845, Marie Laguës had become so attached to the baby that she was reluctant to hand her back to her parents – Bernadette's father and her godmother, Aunt Bernarde, had regularly made the uphill journey to Bartrès, not only to make the monthly payment but also to check on the welfare of this precious baby – and only did so when she found that she was again pregnant herself.

In April 1846 Bernadette, now a toddler aged two years and four months, was back in the crowded confines of Boly mill. The period spent in the fresh air of Bartrès can only have been of benefit to her health – she was to return to that rural scene for another spell in the Laguës household when the family's increasing poverty caused her, at the age of 13, to take up employment as a servant to her former nurse. While she was away from the mill, her mother had given birth to another baby, a boy named Jean, in February 1845. He lived only until April of the same year.

In all, Louise Soubirous brought nine children into the world, of whom only four survived – how tritely we record such a tragic statistic, behind which lie the long months of hopeful anticipation while a new human being develops in the secret chamber of the womb, ending in the death and burial of another newborn or short-lived child. A high rate of infant mortality was an accepted part of the human reproductive process until medical research in gynaecology and hygiene significantly improved the rate of survival. By the time Bernadette returned from Bartrès, however, a third pregnancy had resulted in the birth of another daughter, named Antoinette (shortened in family parlance to Toinette). She was destined to be one of Bernadette's two companions on a day that would change the life of Bernadette herself and of all her family, and that would make the little town of Lourdes as well-known as Paris, Rome or Jerusalem.

Back in the mill, the little Bernadette, while being once more the pet of the houshold – and especially of her father – was already cast in the role of 'heir' in her own family, being the first-born and now having a baby sister. She was still too young, just over four, in 1848 to be able to understand why her grandmother, Claire Casterot, decided to leave the mill with her eldest daughter, Bernarde, godmother of Bernadette, and two other daughters. Bernadette's Aunt Bernarde was, in fact, pregnant and unmarried. The young man in question was Jean Tarbès, son of a local innkeeper. His parents did not approve of his relationship with the daughter of the Boly miller, and delayed their consent to the marriage until late in the pregnancy. Some commentators surmise that Bernarde, now aged twenty-five and already known as a girl who had been passed over in favour of her younger sister, used Mother Nature's traditional method of forcing the consent of the parents on both sides. She eventually did well out of her marriage, inheriting a house and the inn on the early death of her husband. Bernadette's grandmother, however, took the new development as a reason for departing the mill with her three unmarried daughters. She had apparently never been happy with the outcome of her own scheme to find a husband for Bernarde. She still regretted that François Soubirous had not agreed to marry her eldest daughter, and in spite of the supervision of both herself and Bernarde over the miller's young wife, Louise, she could see that the business of the Boly mill was not prospering.

The departure of four adults from the house meant more space and fewer mouths to feed. It also gave the miller and his wife more freedom and privacy than they had enjoyed since their marriage five years earlier. They had always been a truly loving couple and remained so in the turbulent years to come. But the new aura of freedom and joy in the Boly mill was shattered just a year later, on a day in 1849, when François came staggering into the kitchen holding a hand to his bleeding face. He had been working with his tools in a routine dressing of the millstone when one of the stone chips hit him in the left eye. The unfortunate man bore his pain and loss with the stoicism of the poor, to whom such misfortune was an accepted part of their existence; his main worry was that his damaged features might frighten the children and that he might be less attractive to his loving wife. The loss of an eye further reduced his professional efficiency, thus adding to the precarious financial situation at the mill; it also caused him to adopt the habit of keeping the eyelid almost closed, as he appears in the photographs made later by some of the earliest practitioners of that new occupation.

In spite of this physical handicap and the resultant deterioration in commercial prosperity – added to by the unchanging good-natured hospitality extended to what remained of their customers – the family at the mill struggled on, regarded by their neighbours as upright and devout, loving and cheerful, honest and fiercely independent. Bernadette would always maintain in later years that she and her siblings, along with the other children of the neighbourhood, enjoyed a happy childhood. The academic sociologist, studying facts and figures, often deduces that poverty in childhood must imply sadness and misery, resulting in what is termed a deprived childhood; but, as the song says, and as many people know who grew up in such circumstances, 'It ain't necess-ay-rily so!'

The slight stature and congenital weakness that made the young Bernadette more susceptible than her stronger siblings to the effects of malnutrition and unsanitary conditions, had little effect on her strong character and cheerful personality; but Louise Casterot fretted continually that she might lose her frail eldest child. She went to the expense of sustaining her on white bread rather than the rougher maize bread which was the daily lot of the poor, a distinction that caused embarrassment for

Bernadette herself and also, as her sister Toinette admitted in later years, caused some envy in the other children.

In 1851, just two years after the accident to her father, the young Bernadette witnessed the death of her two-year-old little brother, Jean-Marie. The cycle of death and birth was played out once more in the Boly mill when, only five months later, another baby boy occupied the cradle. He was given the same name, Jean-Marie, and he would live into adulthood and be one of those whose testimony and recollections added to the gleanings of Bernadette's biographers.

The year 1854 saw Bernadette achieve her first decade. It also brought on two events of significance in her life, one of which she knew nothing about at the time, the other a social and physical disturbance – nothing less than the eviction of the Soubirous family from the Boly mill.

The first item concerned the Catholic Church as a whole. After it had been a common belief among Catholics for centuries, and a topic of debate among the theologians, the doctrine of the Immaculate Conception of the Blessed Virgin Mary was finally defined as a dogma and an article of faith in 1854 by Pope Pius IX. Like that of papal infallibility in matters of faith and morals, proclaimed by the same Pope at the First Vatican Council in 1870, although dutifully accepted by the faithful throughout the world, the new dogma continued to be a matter of contention among theologians and others until a voice from heaven confirmed the new dogma four years after its proclamation by the Pope: the Blessed Virgin Mary herself used that very title when appearing to Bernadette Soubirous, a poor, illiterate girl living unknown to the Pope and to the world at large in a small town in the south-west of France.

When it issued from the Vicar of Christ in Rome in 1854, the proclamation of this new doctrine went unheard and unnoticed by the ten-year-old Bernadette in the little town of Lourdes. Like her parents and all that lowest of the classes of society, she had never been to school or learned her catechism. Even if she had been told of this new article of faith by a local priest or by one of the town's anti-clerical intellectuals, it would have meant as little to her as an announcement in Greek or Chinese. For a girl who, some years later when she was finally able to attend catechism classes in preparation for her First Holy Communion, was found to know nothing about the Blessed Trinity beyond making the Sign of the Cross, and who was considered by priests, nuns and local officials – mistakenly, as it turned out later and as often happens – to be rather slow in comprehension, religion meant simply devout attendance at Mass on Sundays and holydays, the daily practice of personal and family prayers, and the practice of the virtues of honesty, purity, charity and general goodness as inculcated in her young heart by her parents.

The second significant event of that year 1854, concerned only the miller, François Soubirous, and his wife and family. After a more than usual decline in the income at the mill in 1853 had resulted in consequent problems in renewing the lease, the year 1854 finally brought the inevitable disaster when the miller could not raise the necessary rental. An added humiliation was that a Casterot cousin made an offer to take over the lease. It is said that the Casterot clan in general adopted the attitude, 'We told you so', and blamed the disaster on drink – naturally they asserted that their girl, Louise, had been led into it by that Soubirous husband of hers – while Bernarde, comfortably installed at the Tarbès inn, looked down her haughty nose at the misfortune of her younger sister and the improvident husband she herself might have been saddled with. The Soubirous family moved their meagre possessions to a cheap lodging in the town. François, his reputation as a miller in ruins, was forced to offer himself as a hired labourer to anyone who might need the strength of his arm – the average daily pay for such a labourer was 1.20 francs, that for a horse or a mule 1.55 francs.

Thus, when she was just ten years old, with a tearful farewell to the happy life at the Boly mill, ended the first period in the life of Bernadette Soubirous.

CHAPTER THREE

Hard Times

Like the *spailpíní* or vagrant farm-workers of Ireland in the centuries before mechanisation, there were many casual labourers offering their services to local farmers and others in the marketplace of Lourdes when François Soubirous was forced to join their number. In such a small community, he was already marked down as unreliable and a failure, although honest and willing. His wife, Louise, soon found that if food were to be put on the table, she also would have to offer her services wherever anyone was in need of help in the house or in the fields. Bernadette, now aged ten and considered by both her parents to be sensible and capable, was left in charge of her younger sister, Toinette, and the baby, Justin, born in February 1855.

On days when Louise was working in the fields and the baby cried for nourishment, Bernadette carried him to his mother; then, that undernourished, weary woman suckled him as best she could in the shade of a haystack or a bale of straw. There were days when neither father nor mother had work; on such days, Louise looked after her baby while François wandered around the area looking for work; sometimes, weary and dispirited, he just rested his body and his troubled eyesight by lying on the bed. On such days, while the better-off children in Lourdes trotted along to the Sisters of Charity of Nevers, who had a hospice and a school in Lourdes, Bernadette and her young sister, Toinette, went out to gather firewood for domestic use or to search along by the river Gave for anything, usually rags or bones or bits of metal, that could be sold to a local woman who sold on such material to a bigger entrepreneur. School was still out of the question for children like them, although a few years later they would be allowed to enrol in a special class in which the nuns prepared poor children for their First Holy Communion.

In the Autumn of 1855, poor and rich alike in Lourdes were threatened by an epidemic of cholera. This modern visitation of an ancient plague was first noticed in London in 1830. It crossed the Channel aboard an English cargo vessel and from Dieppe it rapidly spread all over Europe. People who enjoyed a carnival ball in Paris one night in 1832 subsequently fell ill with the terrifying disease for which no effective treatment was known. Within a few days the cases numbered thousands and the fatalities hundreds. The horror soon began to spread all over France, carried mainly by people fleeing from the capital to seek safety in the provinces. Eventually, the epidemic of 1854-55 resulted in 150,000 deaths nationwide. The life expectancy of infected persons varied between twelve hours and three days. The epidemic also added a grim phrase to French colloquial expressions, *avoir une peur bleue,* 'to be in a blue funk' because of the terror inspired when the dying victim's face turned blue.

The first cases in Lourdes occurred early in September 1855. By mid-October, the number of deaths had risen to thirty. As in Paris and other French cities, the richer class in Lourdes sought safety in flight. It is recorded that some of the sick and dying were actually abandoned. The heroes of the hour turned out to be the new Parish Priest of Lourdes, Dean Dominique Peraymale, who had been appointed to Lourdes only the previous March, and the local police Commissioner Jacomet with his assistant, Sergeant D'Angla. Dean Peyramale, of peasant stock, is described as being abrupt and rough in his manner, a man who did not brook contradiction easily, but whose intelligence and charity served as a counterbalance to those off-putting qualities. In the crisis of the cholera epidemic, this good priest brought not only spiritual consolation to the victims of the plague but exerted himself vigorously, along with the two heroic policemen, in applying the only known treatment, a vigorous rubbing down of the sick with straw, followed by efforts to rehydrate the victims.

A few years after their self-sacrificing cooperation during the cholera epidemic, Peyramale and Jacomet, representatives of church and state respectively in the small town of Lourdes, were to find themselves on opposing sides in the furore caused by the report of apparitions at the rock of Massabielle.

When Bernadette began to exhibit symptoms of illness more severe than usual during this period her terrified parents prayed that God would not add her death to those of the other children they had lost; but since none of her family or close relatives were infected by the deadly cholera, it is likely that her severe bouts of coughing and breathlessness, for which she constantly apologised because it kept her family awake at night, were not connected with cholera but were merely an intensification of her constitutional weakness and chronic illnesses. However, a result of this severe bout was the asthma that was to trouble her for the rest of her life. She also suffered continual embarrassment because her parents continued, in spite of their increasing poverty, to buy the expensive white bread for her on account of the weakness of her digestion which could not tolerate the maize bread that was the common diet of the poor and was eaten by the rest of the family. Bernadette used to try to eat her small portion of white bread out of sight of her stronger siblings so as not to arouse jealousy.

Even while the cholera epidemic abated and the impoverished Soubirous family thanked the good Lord for having come safely through, they received news of the death of Claire Casterot, Bernadette's maternal grandmother, on 22 October 1855, fourteen years after the tragic death of her husband which had caused her to set in train the plan that brought François Soubirous acourting at the Boly mill. If there was in the *patois* of Lourdes a proverb similar to the Irish saying that 'God never closed a door but he opened another', the said François and his wife, Louise, must have thought of it when they were told that the woman who had brought about their marriage had left them in her will a sum of nine hundred francs, a sum equivalent to about two years' earnings for an agricultural worker. Perhaps the old lady repented of her hostile attitude to the improvident but loving young couple while she lived at the Boly mill, and hoped now to give them another chance to achieve financial stability and a secure future for themselves and their children.

Undoubtedly, Bernadette's Aunt Bernarde, securely ensconced in her business as a café-owner in Lourdes, together with her sisters, Basile and Lucile Casterot, both now hoping to marry soon, looked sourly at the share of their mother's savings given to their sister, Louise, and her husband, but the recipients regarded it as a godsend. Unfortunately, as often happens with such good-natured but impractical people, the windfall did nothing to improve their business acumen. None the wiser for his previous experience, François Soubirous set off at once in search of a mill for hire. He found one at a place called Sarrabeyrouse, just four kilometres from Lourdes. In spite of his reputation as unreliable and a failure, he convinced the proprietor to accept him as a lessée, and duly, in his illiterate optimism, signed a contract on terms that guaranteed future difficulty. He also branched out into purchasing some cattle, pigs and poultry, with a view to doing something in the farming line. The result was that the Soubirous entered on the occupancy of the mill already in debt, but buoyed up by their unwavering faith and constant hope in the goodness of God.

The venture lasted a year. It was a year when bad weather and failing crops threatened famine in the whole area. Local officials even wrote to the central authorities of the province outlining the desperate state of the common people: the wheat crop was averaging at about a third of the normal harvest, the grape harvest, decimated by mildew for three years, was even worse, and corn was similarly deficient. Because Lourdes was still without a railway connection, no crops could be dispatched and no supplies brought in. Apart from the problem of famine, there was the danger, the local officials warned, of social and political unrest – a strong reminder of what had happened in France just over half a century earlier.

By the end of 1856, unable to find the money to renew the lease of the mill for another year, François Soubirous and his family were back in lodgings in Lourdes, poorer than ever and facing starvation, like many of their kind. Many years later, reminiscing on their plight, Bernadette herself summed up the situation in a comment of peasant pragmatism: 'There were too many mouths to feed.'

With that same peasant pragmatism, Bernadette's parents accepted an offer that would reduce the number of mouths to feed. Bernarde Casterot, Bernadette's aunt and godmother, now the proud owner of the house and inn at the corner of Rue du Bourg in Lourdes which she had inherited through her first marriage, had remarried three years earlier; but in addition to her business cares, she still held herself responsible for the two younger women, her sisters, Basile and Lucile. The former was just then in the same predicament in which Bernarde had once found herself, pregnant and unmarried, with the further problem that the young man she hoped to marry was away on military service and unlikely to be back before Basile gave birth to their child. As the big sister and nominal heir of the family, Bernarde, now also in place of their deceased mother, was in no position to lecture Basile, having set the example of pre-marital pregnancy herself when they lived at the Boly mill with the Soubirous family. Whatever chagrin Aunt Bernarde still felt as a result of her late mother's marital schemes and will, she maintained her affection for her niece and godchild, Bernadette. She now saw a way of showing care for Bernadette and alleviating her own business and domestic cares by taking the twelve-year-old daughter of her sister, Louise, as a general servant in her house and café. If the offer was seen as a sisterly gesture of help to Bernadette's parents in their desperate circumstances, all the better for Bernarde's own reputation in society.

In spite of their personal feelings and their concern that Bernadette did not have the physique or strength for the job – it would entail domestic work as well as serving and cleaning in the café – the Soubirous parents had no choice but to swallow their pride and accept the offer. They knew that at least Bernadette would be well nourished; also, they would be able to keep a parental eye on the situation, while Bernadette herself knew that their door was always open to welcome her home – unless, God forbid, they found themselves without a home and a door to open.

That was exactly how they found themselves a short time later. Early in January 1857, unable to pay the rent of even the cheap lodging where they had taken refuge after the failure of the recent mill venture, they were out on the street, their poor effects piled on a rented cart – a wardrobe, the only item of furniture of any worth, was retained by the proprietor in lieu of the unpaid rent. They were on the verge of joining the many homeless and vagrant victims of the recent bad times when François Soubirous thought of a last desperate resort. The old town jailhouse, only two doors away from the town courthouse, had been abandoned in 1824 because of its insanitary condition. Recently, the neglected old building had been bought by a man named Jean-Pierre Taillade. With the wife and five children of his nephew, André Sajoux – for some reason, the uncle allowed it to be generally thought that Sajoux was in fact the proprietor – Monsieur Taillade now lived on the first floor of the building, while an employee of the nearby courthouse rented an upper room. The ground floor consisted of a dark and fetid room with a stone floor from which the new proprietor had cleared poultry manure and other filth. It had a gaping fireplace and one narrow window looking out on a small yard and a communal cesspool. In former times, the unfortunate people imprisoned for debt had been confined in this dungeon, but it was now considered as unfit for human habitation – it was later described by the Public Prosecutor, Jacques Dutour, as 'a foul, sombre hovel' – except when M. Taillade occasionally rented it to migrant Spanish workers who slept on the floor, often without even a shake of straw for bedding.

It was with the hope of occupying this room – could the cave or stable at Bethlehem have been even half as bad? – that François Soubirous presented himself at the door of the old jail. It so happened that André Sajoux, nephew of the proprietor, was a first cousin of Louise Casterot, Bernadette's mother. When he found the destitute ex-miller Soubirous on his doorstep on a freezing day in January, begging to become the tenant of the dark and cold *cachot* – it was still commonly known as the dungeon – the reactions of André Sajoux were mixed. His main concern was that if he allowed this destitute and starving family to take possession in the nether regions of the building, his kind-hearted wife on the floor above might begin to consider herself bound in charity to share their own meagre supply of food with the new arrivals. The older man, Uncle Taillade, was more worried about the chance of casual rent from foreign workers being replaced by the certainty of no rent at all from the improvident Soubirous. After some discussion, Uncle Taillade came down on the side of Christian charity and family connection. 'We have to take them in,' he said, ' we just can't leave them on the street.'

The cart was unloaded – in later testimony, Bernadette's younger sister, Toinette, recalled their possessions as follows: three beds, a table, two chairs, a few wooden stools, a small cupboard, a small trunk for clothes and things, and some red plates – and Louise set about trying to make a home of the hovel. The fears of André Sajoux were soon realised when his wife, mother of five children herself, provided a little food and also some linen – Louise had sold her own meagre store to buy food. Not that Louise Casterot had forgotten her family pride. 'She never asked,' said her cousin Sajoux later, 'she would have died rather than ask for anything.'

Louise and her husband continued to try to find work, she more successfully in domestic labour than the ex-miller in midwinter when extra hands were not needed on farms or in other areas. Some days, they were both confined to their insanitary cellar, he lying hopeless in bed while his wife tried to make up some sort of a meal for themselves and their three children. Louise, still houseproud even in that dark hovel, washed and repaired the family clothes so much that her neighbours noticed only the fading colour in them. In the houses of the richer folk where she found work, she always appeared neat and clean in her own person, never giving any hint of the grim conditions in her own home. It is said that even the parish priest, Père Peyramale, noted for his charity in spite of his gruff manner, was unaware of the plight of the Soubirous family. Two stories reveal the depths of poverty to which they had sunk.

The five-year-old daughter of Commissioner Jacomet, having proudly completed her first complicated effort in knitting, viz. a pair of small white socks, was urged by her charitable mother to make a present of them to the first poor child they might encounter, 'even if it be a Spaniard' said Mme Jacomet, mindful, perhaps, of those poor migrant workers who sometimes slept in the dungeon of the old jail. The eventual recipient, the first barefoot child they came across, was a local child they did not know – he was Jean-Marie Soubirous, Bernadette's six-year-old brother. It was the same small boy who disturbed the prayers of a young girl named Emmanuelle Estrade in the local church one day. A devout member of the Children of Mary sodality, she was on her knees before the altar of Our Lady one day when she heard a strange scraping noise. On quietly investigating, she was amazed to see a little boy eating the bits of wax he was taking from the candles before another altar. He hung his head in shamed silence on being questioned. However, still silent, he readily accepted the rich girl's invitation to come to her house and have something more nourishing to eat; but the kind-hearted Emmanuelle had to bring the food out to him, as he refused to enter the house. On her invitation, he came back on further occasions, but unknown to his proud mother who would have taken a stick to any of her children if she thought they were disgracing the family by behaving like common beggars. His benefactor, by choice or indifference, remained unaware of the little boy's identity. It was only when later sensational happenings in the Lourdes area brought the entire Soubirous family under the spotlight of public scrutiny that both Emmanuelle Estrade and Mme Jacomet recognised the barefoot boy who had been the object of their charity.

Meanwhile, Bernadette laboured in her many capacities at

her Aunt Bernarde's inn, taking care of her young cousins, washing and mending clothes, and darning and doing needle-work at which she was excellent. When serving as barmaid, she practised her mother's generosity at the Boly mill, filling the measuring cup in such a way that a gulp was left when she had filled the container proferred by the customer. One of her friends later related that Bernadette would say, 'Drink that up, it's good for you!' Wine was a luxury among the poor of Lourdes, but it was regarded as a tonic and a remedy for illness. In their miserable dungeon at the old jail, François and Louise resorted to this palliative for their troubles when they earned any little money, earning for themselves in the process further accusations of being irresponsible and wasting on wine the money they should have spent on food for themselves and their children.

Given the range and variety of the work expected of her, Bernadette's life in her Aunt Bernarde's service was not a bed of roses. It was made more severe by the authoritative style of Bernarde, who was not averse to using corporal punishment when she lost her temper. Bernadette endured such ill-treat-ment, as well as the continual disparagement of her parents, with equanimity and a religious docility. She had been taught to accept all suffering as part of God's will for humanity, and this was the attitude with which she lived from day to day no matter what might befall her frail body and her indomitable spirit. Her ambiguous existence at Aunt Bernarde's place was destined to come to an abrupt end.

Having survived the famine-threatened winter of 1857, the Soubirous family in the old jail might have hoped for better for-tune in the new year; any such hopes were quashed when a new disaster added to their daily misery. On 27 March, the police ar-rived at the old prison and arrested François Soubirous. He was accused of stealing two sacks of flour from a baker for whom he had occasionally worked as a delivery man. The baker himself made the incongruous statement that while Soubirous worked for him, he had found him to be a man of integrity and diligence;

nevertheless, knowing his present destitute circumstances, he named Soubirous as suspect number one in the matter of his stolen flour. The thief or thieves had left bootprints around the scene of the theft, but the boots of François Soubirous, although muddied by the previous night's heavy rain, did not match those prints. Even the setting of the nails was different. The police, however, were reluctant to admit a mistake. In their search at the *cachot*, they had found a very noticeable thick plank of wood. Where had that come from? Soubirous admitted candidly that on the previous day he had been up in the hills near Bartrès – the district where he had often visited his baby daughter, Bernadette – looking for work and incidentally gathering firewood. On his way he had come across this fine plank which had stood for a long time against a wall, unclaimed by anyone. He gladly added this to his collection of branches.

Without any evidence to link him to the theft of the flour, the police readily altered the charge to one of theft of a large wooden plank. Soubirous was lodged in jail and the plank was stored at the town hall, to be claimed by its owner, if any. By an ironic twist, it was never claimed and later came in handy for the municipal authorities: it was to this solid post that the police nailed the notice prohibiting people from visiting the grotto at Massabielle where the young girl, Bernadette Soubirous, claimed to be seeing visions of a young lady dressed in white.

Bernadette's father was released within a week, on humanitarian grounds, said the Public Prosecutor, because of the fact that his family was dependent on him for their survival. That survival became more precarious when Bernadatte arrived home from the town, dismissed by her Aunt Bernarde apparently because of the further ill-repute brought on the name of Soubirous by the conviction of François as a common thief. Her stay at the unsanitary hovel in the old prison was to be brief. During the summer season, both the ex-miller and his wife were able to obtain work of one kind or another; but as the season ended, the grim prospect of a winter of hunger loomed. It became necessary for Bernadette, the eldest child, to look again for some kind of employment. The opportunity was provided by her old wet-nurse in the hill country of Bartrès above Lourdes. Marie Lagües had lost a second son, also named Jean, since the first little Jean for whom the infant Bernadette Soubirous had been substituted at the breast. Now she was anxiously trying to rear a weakly third Jean, who was destined to join the others in heaven before the end of the year. She needed help in the house, and also with the poultry and the sheep. Bernadette willingly fell in with the providential opportunity to again lessen the number of mouths to be fed in the jail dungeon that she now called home. The chance to breath the fresh air of the hills would have been welcome; but she came to Bartrès with an added reason; she hoped that the parish priest there, Father Ader, known for his zeal and piety, would help her to prepare for her First Holy Communion, an event she had long desired but for which it was considered necessary to know certain questions and answers in the diocesan catechism.

As was the case during her spell as housemaid and barmaid in her Aunt Bernarde's establishment in Lourdes, the year spent by Bernadette as housemaid and shepherdess in Bartrès was anything but pleasant. Through all their troubles, the Soubirous family remained a loving and united family, and Bernadette would have been happier in the unhealthy confines of her own poor home than anywhere on God's earth. Her new mistress treated her harshly, and her happiest moments were spent in the fields with her sheep and lambs, moments about which, inevitably, pious legends have accumulated. One creditable story is that once when her father came to visit her, she lamented that something was wrong with her beloved sheep – some of them had developed a green streak on their back. Jokingly, François told her that the grass they had eaten was coming through their back, and that they would soon die. Even when he repented and told her that the green mark was the farmer's indication that they were mature enough to be sold, she was not consoled; she lamented that they were doomed for slaughter anyway.

Troubled in conscience, perhaps, Marie Lagües made occa-

sional efforts to teach the illiterate Bernadette the required theological responses of the catechism. After the day's work, both
teacher and pupil were unfit for such mental labour. Bernadette
stated that it would be easier to push the book into her head than
for her to remember the formulated answers. At times, losing
her patience, the mistress of the house actually threw the book at
the unfortunate girl, shouting that she was so stupid she would
never learn anything. Her brother, a priest who visited regularly,
observing this tirade and some of the rough treatment to which
Bernadette was subjected on other occasions, remonstrated with
his sister; but Bernadette herself never complained. 'She changed
her ways for a while,' she said later of Mme Lagües, 'but then
she went back to her usual style.' To one of her shepherdess
friends in Bartrès, Bernadette made a remark which summed up
her attitude to all the troubles of her young life, and to any that
might be in store for her in future. 'When the good God permits
it, one does not complain,' she said. It is a remark in which many
commentators have seen evidence of the deep spirituality and
genuine holiness of the unlettered young girl who seemed to
casual observers to be merely a naïve and rather simple country
child.

In January 1858 Father Ader left the parish of Bartrès to enter
the Benedictine order. As no replacement had been named,
Bernadette decided that if she were to make her First Holy
Communion the first step was to go back to Lourdes. In spite of
the added burden of having her home again, her loving parents
agreed with her; but her current employer was not at all pleased.
However, when Bernadette, after her regular Sunday visit home
to her family, delayed her return until the following Wednesday,
and then arrived back with the announcement that the Reverend
Father in Lourdes, Dean Peyramale, had agreed to let her enrol
in the First Communion class for poor children at the nuns'
school, there could be no objection. Bernadette said her good-
byes to her employers and to her friends in the surrounding
area, gathered up her meagre belongings, and set out on the
long walk home to Lourdes. On her journey down from the hills,

she passed by the rocky cliff of Massevieille (the old rock), or Massabieille as it had come to be known in the local *patois*. It was while gathering firewood at this rock, less than a month later, that she was to see the first of the series of visions that would make the name of this impoverished and illiterate little French girl known world wide.

CHAPTER FOUR

The Happening at the Grotto

It may seem strange to some readers that Bernadette, now aged fourteen, had not yet received First Holy Communion; however, apart from the fact that she was illiterate and had never been to school, it was still the general custom in the church that children did not receive the sacrament of the Eucharist until their early teenage years, while even adults did not communicate as often as is the practice in modern times. It was left to Pope St Pius X (1903-1914), whose great personal devotion was to the sacrament of the altar, to recall and put in practice the words of Our Lord Jesus Christ, 'Let the little children come to me and don't stop them; the kingdom of heaven is of people like them.' It may be argued, contrariwise, that allowing young children to receive the sacrament 'when they come to the use of reason' also has a negative aspect, not only as regards the level of comprehension of the individual child but in the commercialisation of what is often made into a family social occasion rather than a significant spiritual event in the religious development of the child.

Having agreed to Bernadette's insistent request that she be allowed to prepare for First Holy Communion, her parents also decided that she should be given the opportunity to become literate and to learn French. Although the family habitually recited their prayers in French – the Sajoux family above them used to hear the Soubirous almost shouting their evening Rosary and other prayers – they knew little of the standard language of their nation; their everyday language, like that of all the common people of the area, was the local dialect or *patois*. It would have been of little interest or consolation to them to be told that Napoleon himself, the Corsican who became Emperor of France, was re-

garded as not having fully mastered the French language and
needed secretaries to correct his imperial and other declarations.

Shortly after Bernadette's return from the hillside pastoral
territory of Bartrès, her mother, Louise, went to speak to a Mme
Latour, a local teacher who had a school of her own, with the
idea of enrolling Bernadette. The surname, Latour, is the same as
that of the second husband of Bernadette's Aunt Bernarde, and
that may have been why the approach was made; but even if
there was a distant family connection, it did not affect the impossible financial terms that caused Louise to drop the idea.
Instead, she turned to the Sisters of Charity of Nevers, whose
school in the town included a class for poor children. Bernadette
and her sister, Toinette, were accepted by the nuns and duly
began formal instruction in catechism, literacy, and useful crafts
such as knitting and needlework (their industrious mother had
already made them proficient in such domestic accomplish-
ments).

Inevitably, their school attendance was interrupted by the
bouts of chronic illness that affected Bernadette and by the need
for the younger but stronger Toinette to go foraging for firewood for the hearth and for anything else that could be sold for
a few pence or used in their own home. The worried mother
usually tried to protect Bernadette from the winter cold and fog
by not allowing her to accompany Toinette and other girls on
such expeditions, preferring to leave her to mind little Jean-
Marie and do some housework whenever she herself was fortunate enough to get some work in any house in the town. On one
such day, when neither Louise nor François had a call for their
labour, she reluctantly allowed Bernadette to join Toinette and
another local girl, Jeanne Abadie, on one of their foraging expeditions. On that day the event occurred which was to change not
only the life of Bernadette and her family, but the lives of all the
people of that hitherto insignificant town of Lourdes in the
South of France. The date was 11 February 1848.

That day began like many of the previous days of that month
and of that winter. The gloomy sky added to the cavernous

darkness of the dungeon dwelling of the Soubirous family. François Soubirous, once again without even a casual day's labour, lingered in bed, dispirited and hungry. His harrassed wife, Louise, fretted over the feverish condition of her youngest child, Jean-Marie. The family breakfasted on some soup saved from the night before and re-heated by Bernadette with the last bits of firewood. Then a caller arrived at the old dungeon. It was a girl named Jeanne Abadie, known colloquially as Baloum, her family's surname. She was a vigorous, rough-spoken girl whose mother, like Louise, worked casually as a domestic help. She had come to ask Toinette to accompany her on a search for firewood. On the previous day, they had foraged along with Louise herself, but except for a small amount kept for their own fire, the wood they collected that day had been sold in the town to buy bread.

Perhaps it was a combination of wanting to escape from the sight of her depressed father lying in bed, or to save her mother from the indignity and labour of another day spent in foraging, but Bernadette afterwards realised that she had felt an unusual compulsion to get out of the old dungeon that day and go with her sister and their friend. When she suddenly announced that she would go with them, pointing out that now there was no wood left and also, perhaps, that three would collect more than two, her mother initially refused to allow her because of the cold and foggy weather. Louise finally agreed, wishing to stay with her feverish child, but only on condition that Bernadette wear her stockings inside her clogs – the others had no such comfort – and also her white hood, bought second-hand, washed and darned many times over, but its tough material still offering some protection for the delicate girl.

They soon found that they were not the only poor children of Lourdes searching for firewood in the fields and woods on that cold and foggy day; others had been before them to the nearer fields and riverside meadows where not so much as a rotting branch was to be found. An old woman they encountered – she was washing the guts of a newly-slaughtered pig for her employer – counselled them to go farther on, to the meadow of a neighbouring farmer; he had recently cut down some trees and they might find some small branches. Bernadette, mindful of her father's recent sojourn in the town jail for having appropriated an old plank of timber, objected to her more brash companions, 'Oh no! We don't want to be regarded as thieves.' They had to venture further, along by the mill of the Savy canal and through the adjacent meadow. The miller Nicolau, who knew the Soubirous family well since their time in the Boly mill, let them pass across his meadow with only a shouted warning not to take anything from his own land where poplar trees, recently trimmed of their branches, stood still in the calm, foggy morning.

Further on still, they came to the point where the mill stream rejoined the Gave river, forming a sandy point. On the far side rose the massive rock formation known locally as Massabielle. The place had an unsavoury reputation. It was also cited in a local derogatory saying about an ignorant person who would be described as having only been 'to school at Massabielle!' A large dark cavern, sometimes used as a shelter by fishermen or labourers, was scooped out of its lower part and its cliff face was pockmarked with several caves or grottoes of varying sizes. At this time of the year, it received little sunlight, and winter floods had heaped stones and other detritus in the undergrowth of its nether cavern; but the girls could see that this disreputable locale, frequented by the pigs or cattle of local people, also had a scattering of wood and bones among its rocks.

To get at that store, it was necessary to cross the shallow but freezing cold water of the stream. For the boisterous Baloum and the energetic Toinette, the procedure was obvious; they took off their clogs and threw them across; then, raising their skirts and carrying the few sticks they had already gathered, they went into the water. Bernadette, alarmed by Baloum's exclamations, feared that the ice-cold water would bring on another bout of illness. She remained hesitant and isolated, but called to the others to lower their skirts – she had seem some men working in the distance, and it was an age when modesty was still in-culcated as a virtue in young females. When she called on them to throw some stones in the water so that she could pass over, however, they just laughed and taunted her. Jeanne Abadie test-ified years later that she had even used an uncouth expression when she shouted at Bernadette to manage as best she could while they went on.

While the other two first eagerly collected whatever they could locate among the stones piled up in a slope against the inner wall of the cavern, and then began to venture farther along the bank, Bernadette finally decided on her course of action. She would remove her precious stockingss to keep them dry, and then risk the cold water. She had taken off her clogs and one of her stockings when it happened. What happened? Bernadette was to live nineteen years more, and in that time she would be asked that question over and over again, firstly by her perturbed parents and inquisitive locals, later by hostile anti-clerical offi-cials, wary priests and bishops, learned theologians, nuns both believing and incredulous, journalists and others. No wonder that she eventually became, in her own direct words, sick and tired of people bothering her; no wonder also that, with the pas-sage of the years, and her increasing ill-health, she became con-fused, unable to remember the strict chronology and detail of what happened on that first day and on subsequent occasions. This, in fact, is one of the reasons why her testimony has been ac-cepted as truthful by experts in such matters – a story concocted and memorised, for whatever reason, will be repeated accurately, whereas the detail of a true occurrence usually becomes vague and blurred while the main event itself is indelibly imprinted on the memory.

From Bernadette's many narrations, in oral and written testi-mony, and from the accounts taken down later from her sister, Antoinette, and their friend, Jeanne Abadie (Baloum), the events at Massabielle on that day in February, and their effect on the girls themselves, are well documented. The other two having wandered off from the cavern, Bernadette had sat down and removed her clogs and one stocking when she heard a noise 'like a gust of wind'. She looked around. Behind her in the field there were tall poplars that would sway in the slightest breeze; but they were not stirring. She bent again to remove her other stocking. Again she heard the noise of a gust of wind. This time, looking across towards the rocky hill on the other side of the stream, she noticed that some branches on the side of the rock were moving. They were the branches of a wild rosebush, flowerless now in winter, growing at the foot of one of several cave-like openings in the face of the rocky cliff. While she stared, Bernadette saw a gentle light begin to glow in the dark grotto. Then a form began to appear. It became clearer. Bernadette saw a beautiful young woman standing there, smiling. She was dressed in white from head to foot, with a blue girdle; her feet were bare but adorned with two golden roses, and a long rosary beads was suspended from her right arm. The young girl blinked her eyes tight, convinced that she was imagining what seemed to have appeared in the grotto. When she opened her eyes, the person was still there, beautiful and smiling.

Bernadette now felt uneasy and fearful, but not, she said later, in a way that urged her to run away. Instead, she resorted to what parents and priests had instilled into children as the instinctive reaction to anything that might be from an evil source; she put her hand in her pocket and took out her rosary beads. (Let us pause to ponder how many girls in France or elsewhere today carry similar protection in purse or pocket!) When Bernadette tried to make the Sign of the Cross to begin her rosary, she was unable to raise her hand to her forehead. Then the young lady in the grotto made the Sign of the Cross, upon which Bernadette found herself able to do the same. She began to recite the rosary. While she did so, the lady moved her fingers along her own beads, but did not move her lips. When Bernadette finished her rosary, the lady smilingly gestured to her to cross the stream and come nearer; but the young girl was afraid to do so. Then the vision disappeared.

Bernadette gradually became aware again of her surroundings. The grotto was as dark and gloomy as it had been, just like the other apertures in the cliff face. The dull morning was still windless, the fog had turned to drizzling rain. Although feeling a strange sense of happiness and wonder, Bernadette now became mindful of the practical purpose that had brought her and the other girls to this place. She took off her second stocking and walked across the stream. In doing so, she wondered why her sister and Baloum had cried out that the water was freezing when they crossed over; to her bare feet it felt pleasantly warm. Little did that peasant girl know then that many saintly mystics, when in ecstasy, had felt that same sensation of unseasonal warmth.

When Antoinette and Baloum returned with a good store of wood, they found Bernadette in a strange mood. She seemed immobile, so much so that Antoinette tried to rouse her by throwing small stones at her. They had seen her from a distance kneeling in prayer, and now she seemed to be at it again. Baloum mocked her. 'It's silly to be praying in a place like this – praying in the church is enough!' To which Bernadette replied that praying anywhere is a good thing. When Baloum responded with her former vulgarism, Bernadette cautioned her, 'If you want to swear, go and swear somewhere else.' Next, the other two, still chilled to the bone and with damp clothes, tried to warm themselves by dancing around in the shelter of the cavern. Something prompted Bernadette to protest at this; she already felt that this place had something special and reserved about it because of what she had seen. As they were tying up their bundles of wood, Bernadette wondered if the other two had seen anything. She looked again at the dark grotto, the unmoving bush at its base. Perhaps in doubt, she turned to her companions and questioned them.

'Did you see anything here?'

'No,' Antoinette answered, and then, sensing something in her sister's mood, 'what did you see?'

On her guard now, Bernadette shrugged, 'Oh, nothing.'

Baloum intervened roughly. 'She saw nothing. She just

didn't want to collect wood with us. May will give her a good scolding' (May was a familiar name for Louise, Bernadette's mother). The brash Baloum then declared that she would not face the icy water of the stream again, and set off for home by a route that led uphill around the Massabielle rock. When the Soubirous girls followed, Toinette was astonished that, for the first time ever, the smaller though older Bernadette raced ahead to the top of the slope, while she, the stronger of the two, panted and rested halfway up. When Bernadette came back and offered to help her, an offer indignantly refused, and then expressed the wish to come back soon to Massabielle, Toinette began to sense that something strange must have happened down there by the stream. Her curiosity was matched by the desire in Bernadette's own soul to let someone know about the vision in the grotto. Having got her sister to promise secrecy, she told what she had seen, a beautiful young lady dressed in white, with a blue girdle, a rosary beads, and two golden roses on her feet. Toinette's peasant mind linked the revelation with folk tales of witches and ghosts. Her reaction was to hit Bernadette with one of the branches she was carrying, crying out, 'You're only trying to frighten me!'

In the cold and damp *cachot* that was home, their despondent father was still in bed. While they put some of their newly-gathered wood in the grate, their mother, obsessed with cleanliness and fearful of all kinds of skin infection after her children had been afflicted with lice and fleas left over from the casual occupants in former times, took a steel comb and began on Toinette. Disgruntled, the younger sister objected.

'Why don't you do Bernadette first? You always start with me.'

She decided to get some measure of revenge by disclosing what she had promised never to reveal. When she did so, declaring that Bernadette had seen a white lady up in one of the caves at Massabielle, the mother's reaction was one of frustration and annoyance.

'Oh, no! Not more trouble for us!'

She hauled Bernadette in from the passageway where she had gone to eat her portion of white bread. 'Did you see something? Tell me, what did you see?'

When Bernadette began to tell her, the harassed mother reached for the stick used for beating the clothes in washing and applied it to the two girls. 'You didn't see anything! You saw a white rock or something. I forbid you to go back to that place ever again!'

While Bernadette bore meekly whatever blows and shouts came her way, her sister blamed her for provoking the trouble with her story. The father rose from his bed to make his voice heard. Forgetting the disgrace and bad name he had himself incurred, he declared severely, 'Nothing bad has been said about our people. Don't you start now!'

When Bernadette stuck to her story, her mother began to feel less defiant but more troubled than ever. She knew her own daughter, and she realised that Bernadette was telling the truth, whatever might be the meaning of such a vision. Perhaps, she thought, it had something to do with a dead relative, a soul in purgatory coming to ask for prayers. The discussion was temporarily halted when the girls' rough friend, Baloum, who had not yet heard of the vision, called to the house to bring Toinette with her to the dealer where they would sell the bones they had collected. That evening, before a fireplace now glowing warm with some of the wood they had collected that morning, they prayed as usual. But when Bernadette began to weep uncontrollably, in spite of seeming peaceful and unperturbed, and explained that she felt the desire to go back another time to Massabielle, worry again took hold of the parents. Louise went upstairs to take counsel with Romaine Sajoux. Together, they again questioned Bernadette as she lay in bed. Their combined judgement was that she was a good girl who truly believed she had seen something, but that it was only an illusion, nothing real. The only cure for it was that she should never again return to that gloomy and disreputable place, Massabielle.

While Bernadette slept peacefully that night, apart from her usual periods of coughing and breathlessness, and perhaps saw again in sleep the beautiful smiling vision she had seen that day, her mother probably lay awake for much of the night, hearing those racking coughs as often before, but perhaps fearing now that some mental illness might be threatening her eldest child.

CHAPTER FIVE

Panic at Massabielle

If her harassed mother hoped that next morning Bernadette would have forgotten all about whatever it was she had imagined seeing at Massabielle, the household was not long at its morning routine of lighting a fire and eating whatever little food was available when Bernadette showed signs of fretful thought and unease. When questioned by her fearful mother, she said that something was urging her to go back to the grotto at Massabielle. Vehemently, Louise forbade it, and furthermore forbade any more mention of the matter. She ordered Bernadette to settle down to work at some of the crafts that might bring in some money, like the needlework at which she was so good, and to put all that other nonsense out of her head for good.

For the rest of that day, Friday 12 February, and on Saturday also, Bernadette dutifully obeyed her mother's command. Meanwhile, in the nuns' school in town the girls of the class for poor children were being brought to a high pitch of excitement and curiosity by the possibly embellished accounts from Antoinette and Jeanne Abadie of a beautiful lady dressed in white who had been seen by Bernadette in a grotto above the river at Massabielle. Bernadette herself remained at home, silent and obedient; but in her own mind she was not at peace. She still felt the strong urge to go back to the grotto; also, having on the previous night heard her mother and Romaine Sajoux from upstairs surmising that the apparition, if there was one, could be a troubled soul in purgatory appealing for prayers, she worried that some duty lay on herself not to neglect such a matter.

Being bound to silence and inaction by her parents could not include a prohibition to go and pray in the church late on

Saturday evening. However, Bernadette had more than that in mind. She had decided that her promise to her parents would not be broken if she spoke to a priest in the confessional about what she had seen. The Parish Priest, Dean Peyramale, although of somewhat recent appointment, was already known as a very charitable man but a formidable and gruff personality, a priest of whom the children were in awe and not a little fear. Bernadette knew that one of the curates, Fr Pomian, was usually in the confessional late on Saturday night. He was more gentle in his style, and was actually chaplain to the hospice which the Sisters of Charity of Nevers operated in Lourdes in addition to their school. He was also the priest who, twice a week, taught the catechism to the children of the poor class who were preparing for their First Holy Communion.

When he turned in his confessional to listen to what he judged must be almost the last penitent of the evening – Bernadette was actually the last but one – the tired priest must at first have been puzzled by hearing a childish voice at so late an hour. He was even more puzzled and roused into close attention when he heard this voice saying, in the local *patois* but in so clear a tone that the penitent outside also heard, 'I saw something white, in the shape of a lady.'

A priest like Dean Peyramale would probably have put a sudden halt to the narration and ordered the young girl to go home, say her prayers and go to bed; also, as Bernadette's parents had commanded, not to tell that story to anyone else and to forget all about it. The priest listening to Bernadette, however, was used to dealing with the young children in the catechism class. He knew quite well the official attitude of the church to alleged visions and supernatural visitations; but he decided to let the child go on with her story, and to question her gently, before giving her the appropriate advice. He was in for a further shock. He explained later that when this young girl, beginning to tell her story in detail, said that she had twice heard 'a noise like a gust of wind' but that there was no wind shaking the trees or the bushes, for some reason his mind connected this with the account in the Acts of the Apostles of the coming of the Holy Spirit on the apostles in the room in Jerusalem on Pentecost. The very same phrase is used in the holy scripture – 'suddenly there came a sound from heaven like that of a strong wind blowing' – but the priest knew that this young girl, illiterate and struggling to learn even the rudiments of her catechism, could not know anything of such a link. In spite of this, Fr Pomian stated later that he had still been thinking of how to caution or advise this young girl when a sudden impulse – in the light of subsquent events he considered it to be a direct impulse from God – caused him instead to ask her if she would agree to let him discuss her story with the Parish Priest, Dean Peyramale. Bernadette agreed; but while she herself went home in peace, happy in the knowledge that it was all now in the hands of the priests, she left behind her one very worried priest in the person of Fr Bertrand-Marie Pomian.

The worried curate did not have to wait long for an opportunity to relate Bernadette's strange story to his superior. Later that same evening the two met on a road near Lourdes. The story told by the sincere younger priest must have made some impression on Dean Peyramale; for whatever reason, he did not react with the abrupt negative dismissal of the whole business that might have been expected. Instead, he delivered a succinct verdict that was as orthodoxly cautious and non-commital as any college of theologians could have pronounced. 'We must wait and see,' he said gruffly, and then proceeded to discuss parish affairs, a much more practical and pressing topic.

Events were moving elsewhere that would ensure that the Parish Priest of Lourdes would not have to wait long to see developments that would involve him professionally and personally in the life and story of this little girl, Bernadette Soubirous, whom he did not know at this time, although it is possible that Fr Pomian might have told him something of the troubles of her father.

The day after Bernadette's revelation to Father Pomian was Sunday 14 February. The pupils of the nuns' school were expected to attend the ten o'clock Mass on Sundays, and as they came out of the church on this Sunday a group gathered around Antoinette Soubirous and Jeanne Abadie. They wanted the two who had told them the exciting story to coax Bernadette to go back to the grotto so that they could come along and maybe see something strange themselves. Bernadette herself needed no coaxing; she was torn between the constant urge to return to the grotto and her promise to her parents not to go there and to say nothing more about what she had seen. In spite of her protests, the flock of girls accompanied her to her poor home, declaring that they would ask her mother to allow her to go with them to the grotto. The answer to that group request was what Bernadette had foretold: 'No!'

When they pleaded, Louise got rid of them, perhaps feeling shame that a gaggle of girls should be gathered at the hovel she was ashamed of, by telling them to go and ask Bernadette's father, who happened to have got a day's work in charge of the horses at the livery stables of Jean-Marie Cazenave, a local innkeeper who ran the stage-coach line to Bagnères. The Sunday prohition of work did not apply to keeping horses groomed and ready for the coach; even if it did, poor François Soubirous knew that the good Lord would not hold it against him to avail of any opportunity to put some food on the table for his family – he probably had heard read at Mass that retort of Jesus to the hypocritical Pharisees: 'The Sabbath was made for man, not man for the Sabbath.' When his work was interrupted by the group of noisy schoolgirls, his own two daughters among them, he dismissed them vehemently with the same refusal they had got from his wife at the *cachot*. However, an intervention from Jean-Marie Cazenave, his employer for the day and hopefully for other days to come, softened his dour negative.

'This thing at the grotto can't be bad if it's carrying a rosary,' opined M. Cazenave, urging permission for the expedition; like everyone in Lourdes, he had heard all about the apparition of a beautiful young lady at Massabielle. 'All right!' François growled, 'but be back in a quarter of an hour.'

Bernadette herself led the objection to this. They could not possibly get to Massabielle and back in so short a time. An extension was grudgingly granted. 'Be back for vespers.'

They first reported back to Louise at the *cachot*. She was still worried that the 'thing' might be evil. They countered that they would take a bottle of holy water, a weapon which, in many a folktale, had put evil spirits to flight. Bernadette procured a bottle and some of the others ran to the parish church and filled it there. Then the group, about twenty in all, set off. This time, Bernadette chose to go, not by the Gave and the mill stream as on the first occasion, but up by the forest road behind the rocky pile of Massabielle. The younger ones tried to keep up with Bernadette who seemed to be full of energy as she rushed along; but the older ones, more conscious of the fears expressed by Louise and others that the 'thing' might be evil, hung back in a separate group, pretending they were not as excited as the kids who ran on with Bernadette.

When they arrived at the top of the slope, Bernadette went down so quickly that by the time her young companions, slipping and sliding on the gravelly slope, reached her she was already on her knees, facing the grotto, her beads in her hands. At the second decade of the rosary, her expression changed, her face lit up with joy.

'There she is!' she exclaimed. 'She has her rosary.'

The girls around her, nervous and breathless, could see nothing in the grotto; yet they felt that something strange was happening.

'She's looking at you,' Bernadette said gently.

One of them, Marie Hillot, had the bottle of holy water in her pocket. She plucked up enough courage to hand it now to Bernadette who was still aware of her surroundings. They had rehearsed the standard admonition: 'If you come from God, stay! If not, go away!' Bernadette sprinkled holy water vigorously towards the grotto, calling out the words. The lady smiled. Bernadette continued sprinkling and admonishing until the bottle was empty; the lady continued to smile but did not speak. The

46

girls around her noticed that she became pale and seemed to have lost all awareness of them and of the place. Suddenly they were alarmed when something came hurtling down from the top of the cliff and clattered on the pebbles behind them before bouncing into the River Gave. They shrieked in terror and ran in all directions. A man passing by on the opposite side of the river heard some of them shouting, 'It's following us!' Bernadette's sister, Toinette, and a few others tried to drag her away with them, but they were unable to move her. She was so pale and stiff that they thought she had died in her kneeling position.

The real cause of the alarm was, in fact, a large stone which the rough girl, Jeanne Abadie, who had mocked Bernadette on the occasion of the first apparition, had dislodged from the top of the slope and sent rolling down to frighten the younger children. She now took fright herself, alarmed at what she had done – she could hear some girls below shouting that Bernadette was dead. She burst into tears and ran away, thinking that the stone must have hit Bernadette. While some of the girls ran towards the *cachot* to tell Louise that Jeanne Abadie had killed Bernadette, Toinette and others went in search of someone who would be able to move Bernadette, still kneeling in ecstasy at the grotto. They met the mother and sister of Antoine Nicolou, the miller of the nearby Savy mill. The women came to have a look at Bernadette, and then ran to call Antoine. He was a vigorous young man, noted for his strength and accustomed in his daily work to lifting heavy sacks of grain and flour. He was amazed to find that he could not at first budge this frail young girl from her kneeling position. When he finally succeeded in lifting her, she felt so heavy that he almost fell a few times before he got her to the mill. On the way, Bernadette's face remained fixed in its smile as she gazed at something above them. He related later how he had tried to revive her from whatever it was that was keeping her in this strange state, but she would only go on smiling and gazing at something.

At the entrance to the mill Bernadette woke from her ecstasy. The miller and his mother sat her by the fire and tried to comfort her. 'Did you see something bad at the grotto?' Antoine asked her. 'Oh, no!' Bernadette's pale face lit up joyfully. 'I saw a very beautiful lady. She had a golden rosary on her arm and she joined her hands, like this!' She imitated the gesture of the lady at the grotto.

At this juncture, Louise arrived at the mill, breathless and in terror. Other people from the town were with her; the girls who fled had spread the awful news of an accident at the grotto. Louise was armed with a thick stick, whether to belabour Jeanne Abadie, if she believed the worst, or to punish her own daughter for having caused her to relax her prohibition concerning Massabielle. The culprit in the case had decamped, and Louise was not likely to vent her alarm and exasperation on Bernadette in the presence of the miller's mother and all the others who had gathered there. But her relief at finding Bernadette sitting at the miller's fireside, not only alive and well but looking radiantly joyful and at peace, did not assuage the worry and anger of Louise. 'What are you up to?' she cried, 'you're bringing disgrace on us, getting the whole world running after you.'

When Bernadette protested that she had not asked anyone to go to the grotto with her, the harassed mother renewed her prohibition. This time there would be no change of mind. Never again was Bernadette to go near that place. Poor Bernadette, however, was to suffer more than her mother's wrath because of the disturbance that had occurred during her second vision. On the following day, Tuesday 15 March – it was Shrove Tuesday – she went to school, eager to continue learning her catechism and the arts of reading and writing. The children who had been to the grotto with her had spread the story of what happened all over the school. The nuns, as always, were eager recipients of all the news and gossip of the town. But the Superior of the convent, Mother Ursula Farbes, who up to now had not even known this new girl in the poor children's class, was not pleased with all this nonsense about visions. She approached Bernadette and spoke sternly. 'Well now, have you finished with your carnival antics?' Bernadette remained silent.

More unpleasantness awaited her as she left school that day. A middle-aged woman named Sophie Pailhaisson, who had set herself up as one of the moral watchdogs of the town but who was also, according to some sources, an embarrassment to her husband and an object of ridicule in local gossip because of her outlandish clothes, had discussed the carry-on at Massabielle with a kindred spirit, Sister Anastasie, an unusally cross teacher who was hated by the children. The nun pointed out the culprit, a quiet girl, new in the catechism class, whom many people re-garded as a backward child from a disreputable family – her father was known to be a lazy layabout who had been jailed for theft, and two of her aunts had become pregnant before mar-riage. Sophie Pailhaisson would put a stop to all this superstit-ious chatter about visions at that foul cavern where only pigs used to be seen rooting around. She confronted Bernadette and without further ado gave her a hard slap on the face, accompa-nying this moral lesson with the warning that, if she didn't stop all this nonsense at once, she was likely to end up in jail. It is not known if she added, 'like your father'.

Again, Bernadette said nothing. If she had reacted to such a public assault and humiliation, as other children might have done, by running home in tears to tell her parents, or to her god-mother, Aunt Bernarde, whose inn was nearer to the school, the indignant moralist might have been paid back in kind with a few slaps in the face. As others were to find out very soon, Bernadette was quite capable of response and contradiction that was both precise and vigorous whenever anyone, intentionally or otherwise, tried to alter in the slightest her account of what she had seen at the grotto; but already there seems to have been growing in her devout soul the recognition that the result of what had happened to her there would in some way form part of what she had to endure as the troubles of life. The harsh treat-ment meted out to her at Bartrès by her one-time wet-nurse, like the misfortunes affecting her family, she had accepted with the comment, 'When the good God permits it, one does not com-plain.' One of the leading authorities, Fr René Laurentin, author of a six-volume history and other books on Lourdes, considers that Bernadette was already quite advanced in the practice of true mysticism, which is union with God; but that hers was the kind of mysticism lived in the manner of lowly and uneducated people, the kind that caused Jesus to exclaim: 'Father, Lord of heaven and earth, to you I offer praise; for what you have hidden from the learned and the clever you have revealed to little children.'

Bernadette had to return to school that evening for lessons in sewing and other domestic crafts. Some of the other girls urged her to tell the nun in charge, Sister Damien Calmels, a more gentle type than the Superior, what she had seen. Bernadette, more aware now of her illiteracy and lack of education, protested. 'I don't know how to speak French.' But when the others, eager to satisfy Sister's curiosity, began to gabble their own versions of the story – some even claiming that something had followed them as they ran away – she interrupted to correct them. Poor Sister Damien ended up with a somewhat confused version; but some of the girls began to make snide comments about the pigs' grotto and the lady with no shoes but roses on her feet. On her way home from school that day, Bernadette regretted even more that, on the day of her first vision at the grotto, she had given in to the persistent requests of her sister, Antoinette, and their boisterous friend, Jeanne Abadie, to tell them what she had seen.

CHAPTER SIX

A Question for the Lady

While rumour and opinion, whether cynical or sympathetic, continued to enliven conversation both domestic and public all over Lourdes and its environs, one woman in the town brought developments a step further by intervening in a practical way. Jeanne-Marie Milhet was a well-off woman in her fifties who had grown up as a working-class girl and had risen in society by marrying the elderly man for whom she had worked as house-keeper. On his death, she found herself a property owner and comfortable; she found also that her status of *nouveau riche*, and the manner in which it had come about, proved more of an obstacle to acceptance than the bad reputation acquired in her youth but long since repudiated. She had retained the strong and simple faith of her origins, including an unquestiong belief in miracles and apparitions, and she was much involved in works of charity in the town. Mme Milhet was a leading figure in the Sodality of the Children of Mary, and it was mainly through this that her interest in the news about visions at Massabielle was aroused.

In October of the previous year, 1857, a very pious young woman, Elisa Latapie, daughter of the local postmaster, died. She had been President of the Children of Mary in Lourdes and a close friend of Mme Milhet. Her saintly life and death left such an impression on the people and clergy that the Parish Priest, Dean Peyramale, had actually written about her to the bishop. Some hours before her death, she asked to be buried wearing the blue and white insignia of the Children of Mary.

Madame Milhet heard from her seamstress, Antoinette Peyret, daughter of the local bailiff, the gossip about an apparition seen at Massabielle by the young girl, Bernadette

Soubirous. As soon as she heard about a vision of a young woman dressed in white with a blue girdle – the very colours of the Children of Mary – and with a rosary in her hands, she inevitably connected it at once with the deceased, Elisa Latapie. The problem was that everyone knew how truly devout and totally above reproach had been Elisa's life; so, why then would her spirit appear at Massabielle? Could it be that even so good a life had not been entirely devoid of some small imperfections that required prayers for her soul in purgatory? Or was it that the good Lord was sending her with a warning or a message for the people of Lourdes? With her native peasant common sense, Mme Milhet decided that the only way to solve the dilemma was to go to the grotto with that young girl, Bernadette Soubirous, and find out the identity of the apparition.

Even if she had been told that Bernadette was now forbidden by her parents to return to the grotto, Mme Milhet would not have been deterred from her settled purpose. She occasionally employed Louise Soubirous; so, just as Bernadette's father had been obliged to yield to his employer's plea two days previously, poor Louise had no option but to give her consent when Mme Milhet made it known that she had taken an active interest in the matter. Here are Bernadette's own words, taken from the report of her interrogation by Police Commissioner Jacomet a few days later: 'On the morning of Tuesday 16th, Mme Milhet sent her grand-daughter to call me to her house. I refused to go. She again called me in the evening and this time I went.' One can read between the lines the reluctant permission of Bernadette's tormented mother. 'I told her everything. We agreed to go to the grotto together early next Sunday morning. She didn't have enough patience, however, to wait until the date we had agreed on. In fact, she came to fetch me at home, together with Mme Peyret, on Thursday morning, 18th February. It was very early and I was still in bed.'

It was, in fact, only 5 am and still dark on that winter morning – exactly a week since the first apparition – and the whole family at the *cachot* were probably still in bed. In order to avoid public attention and unwanted company, the resourceful and aggressive Mme Milhet had altered the date of the appointment and arrived at the *cachot* at an hour when others were not likely to be abroad on the dark streets of the town. She was accompanied by her informative seamstress, Antoinette Peyret.

The Soubirous family were aroused by the knocking on their door and were quickly up and about. However delighted Bernadette might have felt at being allowed to return to Massabielle, she must have felt some concern at the instructions given her by the rich woman who had coerced her mother into allowing the visit. Mme Milhet came armed with pen, inkstand and paper, property of the bailiff and acquired for the occasion by his daughter, Antoinette. On the way to the grotto, Bernadette was told that, if and when the lady appeared, she was to proffer the implements and ask that the lady write down her name. This would, Mme Milhet reasoned, clear up the mystery about the deceased Elisa Latapie and possibly let the pious people of Lourdes know the significance of the apparitions.

In her eagerness to get to the grotto, Bernadette ran ahead of the two women. She was already on her knees when Mme Milhet, making an undignified descent from the top of the hill by sliding down on her posterior, arrived breathless and expectant. All three joined in reciting the rosary, but they had only begun when Bernadette said, 'She's there!' The two women could see her joyful smile and her eyes fixed on the grotto which to them remained only a darker area of the cliff that was still shrouded in the gloom of the early winter morning. As with the command drilled into her by her youthful companions on the previous visit, with regard to the sprinkling of the holy water, Bernadette had been coached by Mme Milhet as to the request she would make on this occasion. She was to say: 'Would you be so good as to write down your name?' When they pushed the paper and writing utensils into her hands, Bernadette rose from her knees and advanced towards the base of the cliff, her eyes fixed on the grotto. She stopped near a crevice in the rock-face that communicated with the grotto above. She then held out the bailiff's official writing utensils and said in a clear tone the words she had been taught. Afterwards, she would describe how the apparition moved and seemed to glide down nearer to her, still surrounded by light and smiling gently all the time. Bernadette, nearer now to the apparition than on the two previous occasions, was surprised to notice that the beautiful lady was so young, also that she was small, about as small as Bernadette herself. To her formal request, however, Aquerò, as Bernadette named the apparition – the local word means 'the thing', but is an impersonal and respectful term – still smiling, replied simply, and in the local *patois*, 'It is not necessary.'

This was the first time that Bernadette had heard the voice of the lady, and its gentle tone added to her ecstatic joy. And then she heard the voice again; but this time it was a reversal of the situation between the poor young girl and the beautiful lady. It was a request, made in a gentle tone and using an expression so polite that Bernadette was astonished.

'Would you be so kind as to come here for fifteen days?'

Apart from the invitation itself, with its implication that Bernadette would be favoured with further visions, the courteous manner in which it was expressed was something a poor girl like Bernadette had never experienced in her life. She quickly promised as requested. The lady spoke again. Her voice was still gentle, but her message now was one that would affect Bernadette for the rest of her life.

'I do not promise to make you happy in this life, but in the next.'

While those words were still sinking into her mind, Bernadette felt herself being tugged at and spoken to by the two anxious women who had come with her to the grotto. They had watched her every move and gesture, but they saw nothing else, and did not even hear the words Bernadette spoke as prescribed. Now Mme Milhet could not control her anxiety and curiosity. Bernadette turned to ask them to be quiet or to leave; but while she was doing so the vision faded.

'Why didn't you ask her as I told you?' Mme Milhet demanded crossly.

'But I did ask her!' Bernadette asserted.

'But we heard nothing. Why didn't we hear you speaking?'

'I don't know; but I did ask her.'

'But she didn't write anything. Did she say something?'

'Yes, she smiled and said, "It is not necessary." And then she said, "Would you be so kind as to come here for fifteen days?" '

Like Bernadette herself, the two women must have been surprised both by the content and courteous tone of that invitation. Mme Milhet, however, may not have been totally pleased when Bernadette told her something she would later mention to Police Commissioner Jacomet. In his handwritten report of that first official interrogation, we read: 'Mme Milhet also charged me to ask whether her presence were pleasing to her. Aquerò answered that it was not too displeasing.'

As the darkness dispersed, the three made their slow way back towards the town. Whatever disappointment Mme Milhet felt at not seeing or hearing anything beyond the movements and gestures of Bernadette, she felt satisfied that she had cleared up one thing: if there was somebody appearing in the grotto, it was definitely not the dead girl, Elisa. But then, if it was not Elisa, who was it? The new possibility was one that was already being bandied about in the discussions in Lourdes. Could it be the Blessed Virgin Mary, the holy Mother of God, who was deigning to appear to a poor girl so ignorant and naïve that she herself had no notion of such a marvel and could only refer to the person she was seeing as *Aquerò – the thing*?

When they arrived back at the gloomy dungeon which was the home of the visionary, Mme Milhet had further news for Bernadette's parents. Firstly, there had been, Bernadette told her, another apparition of the beautiful young lady, but she and her seamstress had not seen or heard anything, nor had Bernadette been able to get the lady to write her name or say who she was. However, Bernadette had been requested to return to the grotto for the next fifteen days. Whatever concern the troubled parents might have expressed about such a development was silenced by the imperious Mme Milhet. She had decided, she told them, that in order to avoid having people coming to trouble them at their humble home, she herself would now take Bernadette to live with her. In that way, they could visit the grotto at times and in a manner that would not attract other people.

This peremptory arrangement by Mme Milhet may have been softened with a promise of further work for Louise – she would certainly not have offended the poor woman's dignity by even discreetly leaving some cash to be found later – but there the matter had to rest for the present. As on the two previous occasions when Bernadette had left home, to work for her Aunt Bernarde in town or for Marie Lagüe at Bartrès, her parents were probably glad that she would be more comfortable and better fed than in the dungeon of the old jail, while her absence would leave, as before, one less mouth to feed. As for Bernadette herself, it was the latter reason that made her leave home on all three occasions; she never wanted anything for herself except to live in her own home and with her loving parents, however appalling others might consider their dwelling and circumstances.

CHAPTER SEVEN

Questions for Bernadette

The news of a third apparition, and more to come, spread quickly. Rumour was also doing its work of exaggeration and heated imagination. The idea began to spread that on the last day of the promised fifteen apparitions, some great warning or message was to be conveyed to Bernadette by the Blessed Virgin Mary, now identified by the pious as the lady at the grotto. Bernadette herself, of course, had never given her lady any name beyond the *patois* Aquerò, nor hinted at any message of any kind.

The active interest of Mme Milhet, her participation at the latest apparition, and the fact that Bernadette was now living at her house, had contrasting effects on the attitudes of people towards the alleged visions at Massabielle. The devout parishioners would have been favourably impressed by the involvement of the pious and charitable Mme Milhet. The cynics, on the other hand, and especially the atheistic self-styled intellectuals who met in the local cafés, regarded that very aspect of the affair as further evidence that the whole thing was just another example of superstition in which a stupid peasant child was being manipulated by the clergy and religious fanatics for one reason or another. Apart from these opposing camps, there were two people who took a personal interest in the new development, one for professional, the other for personal reasons.

Bernadette's godmother, her Aunt Bernarde, now an innkeeper in Lourdes, had not hitherto attached much importance to the stories about her godchild having seen something at Massabielle. She was neither of the devout believers nor of the dismissive cynics, but knowing her godchild to be an asthmatic, dreamy, pious sort of girl, she probably felt a tinge of the worry of her sister Louise, mother of the alleged visionary, that the poor girl might now be afflicted with mental trouble in the form of hallucinations. However, when Aunt Bernarde heard that the pious Mme Milhet had been to the grotto and had now taken Bernadette to live with her because, so it was said, the apparition had asked the girl to return for a further fifteen days, she began to wonder what exactly all this meant. Her conclusion was that, if there was any truth in the rumours about visions at the grotto, and if this were to have any importance for anyone, the Soubirous-Casterot family should be in control rather than an outsider like that interfering Mme Milhet.

Aunt Bernarde contacted her younger sister, Lucile, whose fiancé, and father of her child, Dominique Vignes, was now back from military service – the marriage was due to take place at the end of that month. He had often fished in the Gave at the Massabielle area; so, perhaps in view of this and of his military training, he now decided to carry out a reconnaissance of the territory and of the grotto itself. He testified later that, having found and seen nothing, he informed the sisters that all the stuff about visions at Massabielle was a product of the imagination of their niece. He added, mindful, one might hope, of his own part in their unsavoury reputation, that all the gossip in the town was drawing too much attention to the Soubirous-Casterot family and was not likely to do them or their connections any good, especially as the more influential people were now taking a hostile attitude to the story of the visions.

As a business woman, Aunt Bernarde was well aware of these implications; but having astutely considered all such objections, she still felt that the family should take a more active role in this matter of the grotto at Massabielle. She visited her sister, Louise, at the *cachot* and convinced her, to the extent that Louise agreed to accompany her daughter on any future visits to the grotto; obviously, Bernarde was still acting the role of eldest child and 'heir' of the Casterot family. She then went to the house of Mme Milhet, where she informed that lady, as well as her own niece, Bernadette, of her arrangements. However, when

Mme Milhet pointed out that, on the occasion of the most recent vision, the apparition had expressly stated, in reply to Bernadette herself, that the presence of Mme and her friend, Mlle Peyret, was not disagreeable to her, Bernarde grudgingly agreed that they form part of the group that would accompany Bernadette on forthcoming visits to the grotto.

The second person who now took an interest, professional in this case, in the alleged visions at Massabielle was the local Police Commisioner, Dominique Jacomet. He was Chief of Police in Lourdes from November 1853 to November 1858 when he left on promotion. That was the period covering the years leading up to and including the apparitions at Lourdes and their immediate consequences, so that some might say that his posting at Lourdes for that critical period was providential. He was highly regarded in his profession, at Lourdes and subsequently, as a brilliant police officer. He was also on good terms with the clergy; but, although a Catholic by upbringing, he was far from diligent in his religious observance. In this respect, perhaps he was also a providential placement for the case of the young girl and her alleged visions. Had he been either an outright atheist or a truly devout Catholic, he might have been prejudiced in his assessment and investigation. As it was, he was religious enough to believe that if the miracles of the New Testament are true, then God can work miracles at any time; but he was also aware that all through the history of the Catholic Church there have been false visionaries and sensational stories of miracles, sometimes for nefarious ends. When such an event came within his own ambit, therefore, he was likely to conduct his investigation into it in an impartial and unprejudiced manner, sticking to the law and the rule-book and interested only in maintaining law and order.

In his personal life, Commisioner Jacomet was also well regarded by clergy and laity alike. He and his wife were known as a very united couple, their love and togetherness apparently strengthened rather than diminished by the loss of their two young sons through illness; years later, however, when the Jesuit historian, Fr Cros, belatedly began to compile his history of the apparitions, some former colleagues of Commisioner Jacomet in Lourdes recalled rumours that the devoted husband had become involved in a more than paternal care for a young female thief whom he had befriended.

Commissioner Jacomet kept himself well informed of all that went on in his area, and the talk about something strange happening to a silly young girl out at the rocky riverside mound of Massabielle would have reached his ears quickly. He paid little attention to what seemed mere pious gossip until he heard that a wealthy woman had taken the girl to live in her house and was stirring up excitement among her Sodality friends with a story of many more visions to come. The Commissioner thought it was time to examine this business more closely. By the time he took direct action, Bernadette had been to the grotto three more times, going before dawn as she had done with Mme Milhet in order to avoid drawing crowds. On Friday 19 February, only a small group, including her mother Louise and Aunts Bernarde and Lucile, with Mme Milhet, were present. News of this vision resulted in an increase to about thirty on the next day, Saturday 20 February, and on Sunday 21 February, the crowd was over one hundred. On each occasion, Bernadette began reciting the Rosary and soon went into ecstasy, her features shining with joy as she became totally oblivious of her surroundings; many who saw her were convinced that the young girl was really seeing somebody in that dark grotto in the hillside.

One of the onlookers on Sunday 19 February was a medical man from Lourdes, Dr Duzous. Although he was one of a group of unbelieving intellectuals who gathered in a café in the town, he had decided to bring his medical expertise to bear on the nonsense at Massabielle in order to show how science would put a halt to the superstitious excitement of the deluded believers. Having made previous inquiry, he was there when Bernadette went into ecstasy at about six o'clock that morning. He was astonished and mystified at her transformation, but he came near and took her pulse. He testified later: 'It was calm, regular, the breathing easy, nothing in the young girl to show any nervous excitement or anything unusual in the whole organism.' With the others who were present on that occasion, he saw Bernadette's expression change from its usual joyful gaze to one of profound sadness. Tears flowed down her cheeks. When her ecstasy ended, Dr Duzous and others questioned her about this. She explained that at one point, Aquerò had stopped smiling and looked away into the distance. Then, as if she were seeing something that grieved her terribly, her countenance had become so sorrowful that Bernadette began to weep. She asked the lady why she seemed so sad. In her calm and gentle voice, the lady said: 'Pray for poor sinners, and for the world that is so troubled.' Then the vision faded.

On the evening of that same day, while Dr Duzous was recounting his experience to his intellectual friends in the café – his report and impressions would not have been what they expected and were probably scoffed at – Bernadette was undergoing the first of the many interrogations she was to endure. As she came out from Vespers with her companions of the poor children's class, a uniformed constable, Callet, pointed her out to his plain-clothes superior, Commissioner Jacomet. 'There she is!' The heavy hand on her shoulder was accompanied by the invitation, 'Will you follow me?' Bernadette was, in plain language, under arrest. The other children knew what it was all about. They cried out in sympathy, 'Oh, they're going to put her in prison!' Even the adult onlookers were surprised that Bernadette showed no sign of fear at being thus suddenly apprehended by two policemen. She announced calmly, 'I'm not afraid. If they put me in prison, they'll let me out again.'

She was not put in prison. They brought her to the house where Commissioner Jacomet and his wife lived, a large house they shared with one of the local curates, Father Pène, and the local tax official, Jean-Baptiste Estrade and his sister (there was no police station in Lourdes at this time). A crowd of curious onlookers followed from the nearby church. Among them were relatives of Bernadette. All were prevented from entering; but word went quickly to Bernadette's parents at the *cachot*.

Having invited Jean-Baptiste Estrade and his sister Emmanuélite to be present as witnesses, Jacomet seated himself behind his desk and began his interrogation of the small girl in front of him. He began gently, with the formal questions about name, address, family and so on. Bernadette, with her native peasant sagacity, soon saw that these questions were a bit of playacting – this was the man who had caused her father to be imprisoned, making a substituted charge stick where the original one had failed for lack of evidence. She knew that he would have kept himself well informed about everything concerning her visions. She answered all his questions directly and simply. He got her to describe her alleged visions, writing his report while she spoke or answered questions. When his gentle and friendly approach was not productive, he changed his tune. He also became impatient. He tried more devious questions, he even insulted her with derogatory names, he threatened her with prison, he accused her of being in league with her family and other people to make money, citing Mme Milhet and Bernadette's residence at her house.

'I do not live there now,' Bernadette countered, 'I was there for only three days because Madame Milhet invited me.'

At one point, Jacomet's mounting exasperation caused him to raise a hand as if to strike her; only the presence and signalled intervention of Jean-Baptiste Estrade saved him from this indignity and cruelty. He even donned his official cap in order to impress this little chit of a girl who stood there before him, calm and modest, unshakeable despite all his threats and tricks. She even had the cheek to protest, correcting him when he read back to her the report he had written. He was losing face, and not only in front of Estrade and his wife – he knew that his own wife was listening at the door in the adjoining room, as she usually did, along with his subordinates. Even if he knew his New Testament well enough, Commissioner Jacomet probably did not remember just then the counsel of Jesus to his disciples, not to worry about what to say when hauled before magistrates or judges, because the Holy Spirit would inspire them. As a policeman, he prided himself on his ability to pick holes in any alibi, to find the flaws in any concocted story; so, why was he unable to break this illiterate girl who, so his sources – including the nuns at the school – had assured him, was backward and perhaps mentally unsound?

His annoyance with this Soubirous girl, daughter of a no-good thieving father, was compounded by the fact that he knew how this Massabielle business was being ridiculed by his own social class. Even though he did not believe in the story himself, he was loyal enough to his Catholic faith to feel annoyed by those who were making use of it to indulge their anti-clerical bias. Being friendly with the editor of the local paper, *Lavédan*, for which he sometimes wrote himself, he had been given a preview of a cynical article about the alleged apparitions by the lawyer, Bibé, which was to appear in the next edition. It contained gross inaccuracies in its build-up of mockery and derision. The sooner an end was put to the nonsense about Massabielle, thought Jacomet, the better even for the sake of the church itself.

When he read over to her the first version of his report, it was Bernadette's turn to lose patience. 'But you have changed everything!' she cried. To be fair to the man, when he later wrote out a second version, he omitted the alterations he had made in her responses. The two originals are preserved in the archives at Lourdes. They are the first official record of the visions; they also provided material for many of the subsequent interrogations.

As a last resort, the Commissioner ordered Bernadette to promise that she would not go to the grotto again. Her answer was that she had promised Aquerò to do so for fifteen days and must keep that promise. His furious threats of prison had no effect; but he was relieved when the crowd in the street outside began hammering on the door of the house. Bernadette's father had arrived. He was allowed in, but no others. Jacomet ignored Bernadette now and concentrated on making use of the father to control the daughter. François Soubirous needed no coaxing or threats to fall in with whatever Commissioner Jacomet wanted of him. His previous dealings with the Commissioner left him in dread of what might happen to himself and his family if charges of any kind were brought against them. Bernadette had said that she felt as if she were being forced to return to the grotto, and also that she was tired of the whole business. Jacomet knew well enough what the girl meant by those statements, but he quoted them now to her father with the implication that her parents were the ones doing the forcing, and that the poor little girl wished to put an end to the whole affair. Bernadette tried to protest at this misuse of her words, but she was silenced, both by Commissioner Jacomet and her own father. All the poor, illiterate François Soubirous wanted at this stage was to get himself and his daughter out of the policeman's house and safely back to their own poor home. He told the Commissioner that he and his wife were, in fact, also tired of the whole affair, with people banging on their door and tormenting them with questions, and he readily promised that he would not allow his daughter to go near that grotto at Massabielle ever again.

Commissioner Jacomet felt satisfied, albeit ruffled in his dignity. After all, he had achieved his objective. There would be an end to the affair of the visions, and no further danger to peace or law-and-order in his district; just in case, however, he instructed his policemen to keep a close eye on the girl's movements. Although he now believed that Bernadette was neither mentally unwell nor a liar – which meant that she might actually be seeing something out there at Massabielle – so far he had nothing more than that to report to his superiors, and his policeman's mind still suspected that this young girl could be used by others for their own purposes.

Bernadette, on the other hand, went home as calm and unruffled as ever. When her father's sometime employer at the livery stable, Dominique Cazanave, questioned her about the police interrogation, she laughed it all off, even showing some sympathy for the poor Commissioner who had tried to frighten her by putting on his policeman's cap. 'He was trembling,' she laughed. 'And there was a tassel on his cap that kept going ting-a-ling.'

There would be many more interrogations in the days to come. Bernadette would come through them all with the same fortitude and assurance, and with an obvious innocence and clarity of spirit that would convince her interrogators that this young girl was sane, sincere and truthful.

CHAPTER EIGHT

A Test of Faith?

Three days of the fifteen on which Bernadette had promised to
return to the grotto had already passed. On each of those days,
the people with her, growing by degrees from eight to about one
hundred, had seen her in a state of ecstasy but had been told by
Bernadette that the vision did not speak to her. Now Bernadette
was under orders from her father and from Commissioner
Jacomet not to return to the grotto.

On her way to school on the morning after her interrogation
by Jacomet, she could see two policemen tracking her, one of
whom, Sergeant D'Angla, had been put in charge of that surveillance. Sergeant D'Angla was a believer in the dictum, 'like father,
like child', and he openly expressed his conviction that the
whole grotto business was a sham concocted by the convicted
thief, Soubirous, using his half-witted daughter who had the
makings of a future thief.

At the school, Bernadette was subjected to another lecture by
the Mother Superior, who had seen her being arrested on the
previous day, and now congratulated her sarcastically that an
end had been put to her carnival antics and her ridiculous efforts
to draw attention to herself with her nonsense about visions.
The pupils were not slow to imitate the example of such cynics
among their teachers, their jibes and sneers adding to the humiliation endured by Bernadette. Inwardly, however, she was torn
between the constant urge to return to the grotto and her duty of
obedience to her parents – she understood only too well that her
father's injunction was founded on his love for her and his family,
fearing the possible consequences of refusing to comply with the
order of the Commissioner of Police.

After the midday break, during which Bernadette and her sister went home for their meagre meal, they had arrived back at the school entrance when suddenly she felt as if her will and her body had been taken over by some exterior force that wanted to get her to the grotto. She turned and headed in that direction. So did Sergeant D'Angla and his colleague. Alerted by someone, Aunts Bernarde and Lucile quickly pursued the growing group; by the time Bernadette knelt at the grotto, nearly one hundred people were there. Sergeant D'Angla took up his position beside her, watching every movement. Another observer was Mlle Estrade, the lady who, on the day before had been present with her brother, Jean-Baptiste Estrade, in the office of Commissioner Jacomet when he interrogated Bernadette. She had been so impressed by Bernadette's behaviour during that ordeal that she had decided to come and see for herself what went on at the grotto.

As usual, Bernadette took out her rosary and began to pray, imitated by those present who were believers. After some time her face changed, but not as usual. Her expression was sad and worried, not at all ecstatic. Sergeant D'Angla interrupted her repeatedly, 'Well, do you see her, do you?' There was no vision that day. Sergeant D'Angla mocked the distressed girl and called out to the crowd, 'There you are, it's a lot of nonsense and superstition! My policeman's cap frightened the apparition away!'

Any cynical observers who had never seen Bernadette in ecstasy went away confirmed in their mockery, while the pious believers, even those who had seen how the vision transformed Bernadette on previous occasions, were puzzled and disappointed. Why did the vision not appear on this and on one subsequent occasion? People did not notice at the time that, when graciously asking the girl to come to the grotto for fifteen days, the Lady had made no promise that Bernadette would see her on each or even any of those days. Perhaps the non-appearance was a test, not only of Bernadette's faith, but also of that of all those others who were now aware, to whatever degree, of the events at the grotto. Bernadette's personal reaction was to seek some fault in her own conduct. She murmured plaintively, 'I don't know in what way I have failed her.' Her aunts led her away from the mockery of the cynics and the comments of the disappointed pious believers to the security of the nearby Savy mill where she had found refuge on previous days.

One can imagine Sergeant D'Angela reporting triumphantly to his superior officer, 'No vision, sir! You put a stop to the games at the grotto.'

Commissioner Jacomet was not so sure. If the visions and the ecstasy were a fake, the girl could surely have put on a repeat performance today, especially for the benefit of the police who were present. Instead of which, as this naïve and biased sergeant had reported, she was obviously disappointed and distressed at the non-appearance of her vision. And why, on her way obediently to school in the afternoon, had she suddenly turned around to head for the grotto, thus openly defying his order and disobeying her own parents? Sergeant D'Angla was commended on his good work; but, to his surprise, he was ordered to continue his surveillance of the Soubirous girl.

Bernadette was worried in conscience that her disobedience to her parents might have been the cause of the non-appearance of her beloved Aquerò. When, after the first apparition, her parents had forbidden her to go to the grotto, she sought counsel in the confessional of Fr Pomian, one of the curates. Now she went to the same counsellor and presented him with her problem: was she to obey the vision at the grotto, to whom she had made a solemn promise, or was she to obey Commissioner Jacomet, who had threated her and her parents if she kept her promise to Aquerò? Father Pomian later testified that, having conscientiously considered her dilemma, something in his soul seemed to make the decision for him. What he said to her was: 'They do not have the right to stop you.'

On that same evening, some of the civil and legal authorities of Lourdes had convened a meeting to discuss the affair of the alleged visions. They included the Mayor Lacadé, the Public Prosecutor, Jacques Dutour, and Commissioner Jacomet, with

Sergeant D'Angla as a recent witness of events. Their conclusion proved a setback for Commissioner Jacomet. The Mayor himself summed it up thus: 'The prohibition has no legal basis. Public opinion is on the side of the little girl, and they will not fail to blame us if we take action against her. She must be kept under surveillance, but it would be a mistake to repress her.'

Next morning, Tuesday 23 February, Bernadette resumed the pattern of her previous visits. At 5.30 am she was on her way to the grotto where a crowd of about 150 people gathered. For the first time, these included not only the common people of Lourdes and its surrounding area, but a group of some of the intelligentsia of the town, some influenced by the report of Dr Duzous who had seen Bernadette in ecstasy, others like the lawyer, Dufo, and Jean-Baptiste Estrade, the tax-collector who lived in the same house as Commissioner Jacomet, coming reluctantly as escorts, on this dark winter's morning, for Mlle Estrade and some other ladies whose interest she had aroused after her observance of Bernadette on the previous day. Most of the ladies, just like Estrade and Dufo, came incredulous. They saw Bernadette in ecstasy, and Estrade, at least, went away as firm a believer as his sister. Like her, he had seen Bernadette's face previously only when she stood before the Commissioner of Police in his office. When he saw that same face transformed in ecstasy, he could only say later to his friends at the café that her beauty at that moment surpassed any of the beauties he or they had ever seen in the theatre at Bordeaux. 'That child,' he asserted, 'has a supernatual being in front of her.'

On the next day, Wednesday 24 February, there were almost 300 people waiting at the grotto when Bernadette arrived – already the numbers were so large that people were occupying every possible vantage point above and around the grotto and the lower cavern. Bernadette went through the same motions, first praying and then going into ecstasy as she smiled at the vision in the grotto. Today, however, she added something else to her behaviour. Seeming to follow some instruction, she moved forward on her knees over the uneven and stony ground, then she threw herself on her face and kissed the muddy earth. On seeing this her Aunt Lucile, still only eighteen years old, who had been kneeling beside Bernadette, collapsed in a faint. When the vision ended, and Lucile had been revived, Bernadette explained her unusual behaviour. The vision had asked her to do so as a penance, and to pray to God for the conversion of sinners.

The apparition on the next day, Thursday 25 February, was to be one of the most significant of the series, both in itself and for its lasting consequences

Is she mad?

In many households all over the Catholic world today, a bottle or a water-font contains water from the spring that gushes from the ground in the arched cavern under the grotto of Bernadette's visions. Pilgrims at Lourdes can queue to see the spring, now protected by a transparent cover, and fill their bottles at a series of taps nearby to which the water is conducted. They can also, whether able-bodied or otherwise, present themselves for aided immersion in baths located in a building on the other side of the grotto; the water for these baths also comes from the spring. When Bernadette arrived at the grotto on the dark morning of 25 February 1858, no such spring was visible, nor had anyone ever seen water issuing from the ground there, although the water that drips from the rocky hill of Massabielle made the area muddy.

On that morning, people were heading to the grotto from around 2 am, their lanterns flickering in the darkness. Among them were Mme Jacomet, acting as civilian spy on behalf of her husband. The enthusiasm of Jean-Louis Estrade, a recent believer, and his sister, Emmanuelite, had aroused the curiosity of some of the most incredulous among their friends. Even the fashion-able daughters of the hotel-keeper Lacrampe, impressed by the assertion of Jean-Louis that the Soubirous girl in ecstasy was far more beautiful than a famous actress they had all seen in Bordeaux, were curious to the extent that they were willing to rise at such an unearthly hour and endure the crush of the com-mon mob around the grotto.

There were nearly 400 people crowding at all points when Bernadette herself arrived at around 6 am, wearing as usual the

large white hood Louise had provided long ago as a protection
for her frail daughter. She found it difficult to get through the
crowd until Sergeant d'Angla, forgetting he was on surveillance
duty for Commissioner Jacomet, took charge and cleared a way
for her. The crowd hushed into a silence that was respectful and
expectant as Bernadette, in her usual place, lit her candle and
began her rosary. Soon she was in her usual state of ecstasy, but
after a short while she removed her hood and handed it, with
her candle, to a girl kneeling near her. Then she performed the
penitential exercise of the day before, moving on her knees over
the sharp pebbles up the slope towards the wall of the cavern.
The awed crowd made way for her as she now and again fell on
her face to kiss the ground.

When she came to the crevice in the wall of the cavern which
was like a vertical chimney that led up to the niche of the apparition, she seemed, as often before, to be in conversation, although
the people crowding around heard no sound. Then she turned
around and came back, obviously instructed, and crawled on
her knees towards the river, her agility amazing the people who
made way for her. But then she halted again, looking back with
a puzzled expression towards the grotto. As if receiving further
instructions, she rose and began to walk towards the back of the
cavern, to the point opposite the niche of the apparition. She
bent and seemed to be searching the ground, a mixture of pebbles and mud. She turned and came out again, looking towards
the grotto as if asking and listening. She went back to the same
corner, knelt and inspected the muddy soil. Seeming puzzled
and disturbed, she glanced back at the grotto, nodded, and then
began to scrape the ground with her right hand. When she had
made a small cavity in the ground, she took some of the reddish
mud from the hole, raised it to her face as if to wash or drink,
and then threw it from her, grimacing in disgust. She seemed to
be trying to drink some of the liquid mud, but unable to over-
come her repugnance. At the fourth attempt, she managed to do
so. After which she looked around in the same area, plucked
some herbs, and ate a few leaves.

When she rose from her knees, turned and came out from the shelter of the cavern, those near her could see that her face was soiled with the reddish mud. Those farther off could hear the muttering of the hostile cynics. 'She's crazy!' Mme Jacomet was heard to laugh, while Elfrida Lacrampe, the hotelkeeper's daughter, who had endured such unusual early rising and physical discomfort in order to see the beautiful face described by Estrade, snapped at him, 'You brought us out here to see that silly little shithead!' Estrade himself was mystified and confused. He knew what he would have to face from the anti-clerical intelligentsia in the café that evening.

Bernadette explained her weird actions to those who gathered around to question her (she repeated this in later written testimony). She said: 'Aquerò told me to go and drink at the fountain and wash in it. I could not see any fountain; so, I went to drink at the river. She said that it wasn't there I had to go and pointed with her finger to show me where the fountain was.' (The dialect word, *hount*, used by Bernadette, corresponds exactly to the Latin word *fons*, fountain.) 'When I found some water it was more like mud, only as much as I could hold in my hand. I tried to drink it three times and threw it away because it was so dirty. The fourth time, I managed to drink some of it.' To questions as to why such strange behaviour was requested by Aquerò she could only reply, 'I don't know; she didn't tell me.' But, as with the less abnormal actions on the previous day, she said that it was all for sinners.

The crowd began to disperse, some jubilant and making comedy of the whole affair, but most of them despondent and puzzled. The few who stayed to pray at what was already regarded as a holy place noticed in the dawning light of day that the small muddy hole scraped out by Bernadette had become a small pool of clear water. By the afternoon, people coming to the grotto saw that trickles of water were now flowing from it. They scooped it out more, hearing the noise of gurgling water below. The more they dug, the more it flowed, growing clearer as it did so. Some people drank the water, finding it easier to do so than

Bernadette, finding it also as cold and refreshing as the water from any spring in the nearby mountains. Some commentators later saw in the muddy water changing to a clear spring a symbol of the conversion from the mire of sin to the clarity of repentance.

That is the clear spring water that has been flowing in abundance, ever since 25 February 1858, from the ground beneath the rocky cavern at Massabielle. Nowadays, the cavern having been cleared of its sloping pile of earth and stones, the ground is level and a never-ending line of pilgrims, some in wheelchairs, passes slowly by to view with reverence the crystal-clear water that constitutes an unfailing source of supply for the nearby taps and baths.

The appearance of this gushing water, following on the strange behaviour of Bernadette, was a phenomenon that all those present had seen, unlike the actual apparition in the grotto which some believed the young girl, Bernadette, was seeing, while others continued to regard her as mentally unbalanced or a dupe of religious fanatics. When stories began to spread of curative powers in the water that had begun to pour from the earth at Massabielle – on the very first day, a few people took home bottles and other vessels filled from the spring, the first of many millions who continue to do so – some professional chemists took samples in order to analyse it. The first verdict was that the water was unsafe for drinking. Another expert contradicted this and stated that the water had beneficial mineral qualities, just like the water at the fashionable spas of France and other countries. This second verdict was greeted with enthusiasm by the mayor and business people of Lourdes. Their vision was more material than what the young Soubirous girl claimed to see; the town of Lourdes would attract lots of people seeking cures for their various ailments, hotels and general business would boom. Their vision proved right, but for reasons other than they had envisaged, although initially they suffered disappointment when a third and more scientific analysis reached the final verdict: the water in the spring at Massabielle was no dif-

ferent from that in any other spring in the Pyrenees or elsewhere. It had no special properties, harmful or beneficial. One
could drink it or wash in it with the usual benefits, viz. it would
serve to quench thirst or to promote cleanliness. All subsequent
analyses have confirmed that verdict.

The strange events of the morning must have been discussed
all over the town during that day. Bernadette probably suffered
more humiliation and mockery from nuns and pupils at school.
She was to suffer more before the day was out. In the evening, a
policeman came knocking at the door of the Soubirous home. He
had a summons for the girl, Bernadette Soubirous, from the
Public Prosecutor in Lourdes, Jacques Dutour. She was to present herself at his office at 6.00 pm for another interrogation.

On that day, Bernadette's father had been fortunate in getting a day's work from M Cazenave. He had driven a coach to
Tarbes, where it was market-day, and would be home quite late.
Bernadette's mother, Louise, sent word to her cousin, André
Sajoux, who was working at a nearby quarry, begging him to
come and accompany Bernadette and herself to the office of the
Prosecutor. He rushed home to the old prison which was his
home also, and changed into his Sunday best. At the Prosecutor's
office, however, when he identified himself, he was debarred
from entry and withdrew to the refuge of an inn across the road,
owned by another of his relatives.

Prosecutor Dutour had the report of Police Commissioner
Jacomet before him when he began to interview Bernadette. He
had the same attitude as Jacomet to the events at the grotto, but
apparently hoped that his legal mind would find more subtle
ways to trap this girl into an admission of complicity in a
scheme of deception, or else to show clearly that she was, as
many of his class believed, unstable and suffering from hallucinations. After nearly two hours of effort, during which he kept
Bernadette and her mother standing while he sat behind his
desk writing – Bernadette, although illiterate, noted that his
writing deteriorated as he became more agitated with her answers; later, at home, she made fun of the flurried way in which

he crossed out words and missed the inkwell when trying to dip his pen – the Prosecutor had achieved no more than Commissioner Jacomet. When, as a last effort to frighten her, he called to a policeman present, 'Go and tell the Commissioner to come and have this girl put in prison,' Bernadette remained calm but her poor mother burst into tears. At last, the Prosecutor remembered common manners and decency. He pointed to some chairs. 'You can sit down.' Sobbing, Louise collapsed into a chair. Bernadette, however, felt the offence in his condescending tone. 'No,' she snapped, 'I would soil it.' So, she promptly sat on the floor, 'just like tailors do!' she laughed later.

The interrogation came to an end when André Sajoux and his friends from the café, fortified by a few drinks, came banging on the door and the window shutters, shouting to be admitted. The Prosecutor had no option but to release the women, who were taken to the café to be revived with some refreshment. Jacques Dufour sent an official report of the interview to his provincial superiors, but the more detailed and valuable evidence in his scribbled notes never became available for historians. He apparently destroyed them when further sensational developments at Lourdes made all those, like himself, who had initially humbled and despised the poor and illiterate visionary, an object of dislike and recrimination.

CHAPTER TEN

Signs and Wonders

On the morning of 26 February, the day after the appearance of the spring – some people were already calling that in itself a miracle – and the interrogation by the Public Prosecutor, there were divided opinions in the Soubirous home. Bernadette felt her usual compulsion to keep her promise concerning the fifteen days. Her parents, however, feared the wrath of the Prosecutor, his threats being now added to those of Commissioner Jacomet. Aunt Bernarde, who was now taking a more active part in all that concerned the apparitions, came down on the side of her godchild and said that, were she in Bernadette's place, she would go to the grotto. The decision of the Casterot 'heir' still carried weight. Bernadette put on her white hood and they set out.

There were about 600 people gathered when Bernadette arrived. She went through her customary ritual, reciting the rosary and performing the penitential exercise of moving about on her knees over the stony ground. Just as on the day after her interrogation by Commissioner Jacomet, there was no apparition. Another test of faith, perhaps, for herself and for the people gathered there, or an indication of disapproval and a warning from Aquerò herself for the officials who were treating the innocent visionary with such cruelty.

Having washed her face and hands at the spring, now clearer and stronger, Bernadette was taken once again to the refuge of the nearby Savy mill. As on the previous non-appearance, her only concern was that she must have displeased the lady in some way.

The next morning, 27 February, her joy was all the more as an even larger crowd saw her transformation into ecstasy on the appearance of her beloved Aqueró. An observer at this apparition was Antoine Clarens, headmaster of the secondary school in Lourdes. Like some of the other intellectuals, he had hitherto refrained from mixing with what they considered the deluded pious mob at Massabielle. Now he came at the request of his friend and patron, the Prefect of the province, to gather material for an account of the affair that would be an intelligent, objective, and of course impartial analysis of this latest manifestation of superstition and religious hysteria.

Whatever he made of Bernadette's strange appearance when she gazed in ecstasy at the niche in the cliff and seemed to converse with whatever it was she was staring at, the condescending pedagogue from Lourdes was as disgusted as others of his kind had been when he observed her crawling around on her knees and falling occasionally to kiss the ground. He presented himself at the Soubirous home later that day to interview the girl herself. She explained her strange actions as she had done before: 'It was in penance, first for myself, and then for others.' Like everyone who did so, whether believer or cynic, M Clarens was impressed by the young girl's natural charm and complete candour. Also, like those interrogating officials in Lourdes, he came away from the interview a puzzled and disconcerted man, having failed totally to shake Bernadette's absolute faith in her visions or to find any intellectual incapacity in this illiterate peasant girl. His verdict was no different from that of Dean Peyramale, Parish Priest of Lourdes: 'We must wait and see how things develop.'

Already there were stories of miraculous cures associated with the water of the spring at the grotto. Bernadette, however, in all interviews and interrogations, never spoke about miracles and insisted that she knew nothing about such signs and wonders; all she could do was to repeat what she had already told, and would again have to tell so many times, what she had seen and heard at the grotto since that fateful 11 February when she heard a strange gust of wind and turned to see a beautiful young woman appearing in the brightening niche in the cliff face at Massabielle.

The authorities were growing more concerned about public safety at the grotto because of the increasing crowd, and although there were no reports of violence or aggressive behaviour, they still feared the possible consequences for law and order on the final day of the fifteen, 4 March, if the crowd became hysterical because of some message or warning from the 'vision', or became riotous as a result of disappointment. A further interrogation of the Soubirous girl was decided on. This time it would be by a higher authority still, Judge Ribes, the magistrate. As Bernadette was leaving the church after High Mass on Sunday 28 February, with her companions of the hospice school, she was arrested and brought before a tribunal consisting of Judge Ribes, Prosecutor Dutour and Commissioner Jacomet. The sister who was in charge of the children protested to no avail, and then, in tears, went off to report to the Mother Superior.

The interrogation went through the same process as the previous two, and came to the same conclusion, Bernadette calm and unshaken, the Judge, like his fellow officials, frustrated and angry. Again, Bernadette refused to promise not to return to the grotto – she had promised Aquerò and must keep her promise. To threats of prison, she replied that they could not keep her there. They knew that they could not even invoke any law to stop her from going to the grotto. Their frustration was added to when they were interrupted by someone demanding the immediate release of the girl. This time it was not some humble and timid relative, but Mother Ursula, the Superior of the Convent, who, like some of the other nuns, had herself subjected Bernadette to sarcastic hostility since the beginning of the events at the grotto. Was her intervention here an indication of a change of attitude or merely a declaration to those secular authorities that this was a matter to be left to the jurisdiction of the church? Whatever its cause, poor Bernadette had felt more confident and at ease before the Judge and his colleagues than she

did when being publicly conducted back to her Sunday catechism class by the formidable Mother Ursula.

Next day, Monday 1 March, there were people arriving at the
grotto by midnight, carrying lanterns and seeking a point of
vantage from which they would be able to see Bernadette when
she arrived in the early morning. As the hours went by, the
crowd increased to over 1,500. People were quiet and respectful,
praying individually or in groups. Among them there were soldiers from the local fort, encouraged to come by their command-
ant who was a friend of Jean-Baptiste Estrade and had been present with him at a previous apparition. Also present that day,
for the first time, there was – a priest! It was well known that
Dean Peyramale had forbidden his curates to go near the grotto
or to express any opinion in public except the cautious official
attitude of the church to any alleged visions or signs. However,
this priest, Fr Antoine Dezirát, was not one of the local curates.
He was 28 years old, recently ordained, and staying with his
parents while he awaited an assignment from the bishop. He
was aware of the injunction of Dean Peyramale, but his conscience allowed him to consider that this applied only to the
priests under Peyramale's direct authority.

The crowd, wrongly but joyfully interpreting his presence as
a sign of official church approval, made way for the young priest
until, to his surprise, he found himself pushed to the very front.
Bernadette arrived, accompanied by both parents for the first
time, and they had to assist her in making her way through the
crowd because so many people wished to touch her. The priest
later wrote an account of Bernadette in ecstasy. 'Her smile is beyond all description. No artist or actress could ever reproduce
her charm and grace. The joy and the sadness on her face, one
succeeding the other with the speed of lightning. I had watched
her with close attention when she arrived at the grotto. What a
difference between the girl she was then and the girl I saw at the
moment of the apparition! Respect, silence, recollection reigned
everywhere. Oh, how good it was to be there! I thought I was in
the vestibule of paradise.'

If he had stayed on after the apparition, Fr Antoine Dezirát might have had another story to tell for the rest of his life – he could have witnessed the first cure that would gain official church recognition, but only after a long process of episcopal inquiry and medical evidence. Bernadette and most of the crowd had departed when a woman who had been among the vast crowd made her way towards the spring in the shade of the cavern. She was a peasant named Catherine Latapie and she lived seven kilometres from Lourdes, at Loubajac. She had two small children and she was nine months pregnant. Nearly two years earlier, in October 1856, she had suffered an accident. Climbing a tree to knock down acorns for her pigs, she had fallen and broken an arm. The doctor succeeded in setting the arm, but she was left with two fingers on her right hand paralysed and doubled up. She was unable to use her right hand, with the result that she could no longer spin or knit or do any other such work that would have been useful to her own family and perhaps earn a little money besides.

In the middle of the night, this woman felt a strong impulse to go to the grotto at Lourdes. She took her two young children with her and walked through the dark night until she reached the grotto. There she witnessed the ecstasy of Bernadette. She waited until almost all of the crowd of over a thousand had dispersed; then she made her way to the cavern and to the spring, source of the little stream that was now flowing to the nearby River Gave. She plunged her hand into the ice-cold water. Suddenly, she felt a strange mood of peace and calm; also, she felt her crippled fingers moving. She lifted her right hand from the water – the fingers were moving as if they had never been injured. While she was attracting the attention of people around her by crying out her thanks to the Blessed Virgin Mary, she felt a warning labour pain and changed her prayer to one for help to get home safely. Grabbing her two small ones, she set out on the long walk back to Loubajac. She had barely arrrived at her house when she gave birth to a sturdy son. He was destined to become a priest.

During her ecstasy on the next day, 2 March, Bernadette was seen to be, as often before, in conversation with the apparition. More than 1,500 people were crowded around her, some even hanging out of every nook and cranny in the cliff of Massabielle, others occasionally pushed into the shallow stream by the press of people behind them. None heard any sound from the moving lips of Bernadette or from the grotto towards which she was gazing. When the ecstasy finished, however, Bernadette revealed a message from Aquerò, a message that was also a command: 'Go and tell the priests that they are to build a chapel here and that people are to come here in procession.' It is worth noting, in view of later developments, that the word *processiou* in the local *patois* means *pilgrimage* in the modern sense.

As soon as she could make her way through the crowds, Bernadette set out to fulfil that mission. Whatever fear she might have felt of daring to call at the house of the gruff Dean Peyramale was quenched by her loving obedience to the lady of her visions.

Unknown to Bernadette, however, some of the devout people who had heard – or perhaps misheard – her revelation, rushed along to the house of the Parish Priest. They had interpreted the words about a procession as obviously having a meaning for the big day, 4 March, the final day of the fifteen, something Bernadette had not said. Dean Peyramale had previously listened closely to anything the devout believers in the apparitions had told him. Like Commissioner Jacomet, he was keeping himself closely informed of developments, while stringently maintaining a public attitude of neutrality; but when some of these same pious parishioners came rushing now to tell him the great news, viz. that the lady of the visions required him to organise a procession to the grotto for Thursday next, the good man did not mince his words. Those first informants had been sent packing with his angry refusal burning their ears when Bernadette arrived at his door, accompanied by her Aunts Basile and Lucile

The reception they got almost caused Bernadette to forget the message she had so diligently memorised. Dean Peyramale greeted her with heavy sarcasm.

'Oh, so you're the one who goes to the grotto and says she sees the Holy Virgin?'

Bernadette answered simply. 'I did not say that it is the Holy Virgin.'

'Then who is it?'

'I don't know.'

More questions followed, together with some barbed asides to Bernadettes's aunts. One of them, Aunt Basile, as well as her older sister, Aunt Bernarde, had been thrown out of the Sodality of the Children of Mary because of their pre-marital pregnancy; so, there was no mistaking the force of the priest's tirade about a family that was bringing trouble and disorder to the parish. Having totally rejected all talk of a procession on Thursday – he would have needed long notice for any such event so that he could seek permission from the bishop – Dean Peyramale ordered them to leave his house and to leave himself in peace in future. In his own soul, however, he was a troubled man, especially when he thought again of how impressed his two curates were by that young girl and her alleged apparitions. He could also see for himself that happenings at the grotto were having a beneficial effect in his parish in the matter of religious observance. How could this good result come from something that was not good? There was some line in the gospel about that.

Not far from his door, Bernadette remembered that she had not even mentioned the chapel the lady had requested. Her aunts flatly refused to go back, and counselled Bernadette likewise; so, all three made their way back to the *cachot*. There, further discussion took place, joined in this time by Dominiquette Cazenave, an ardent believer in the visions; and sister of the man for whom François Soubirous worked now and again. A parishioner of good standing with the clergy, Dominiquette volunteered to go herself and request a further meeting between Bernadette and Dean Peyramale. She came back with the news that he had agreed to meet them both at 7 pm that same evening. When they arrived, they found that several other priests, including Bernadette's gentle confessor, Fr Pomian, had been assembled by the cautious Dean Peyramale to act as witnesses and to form what was almost a clerical board of inquiry.

Bernadette managed to convey the second part of the request, a chapel to be built at the grotto; but she was so confused by the harshness of her previous reception, as well as by the gathering of priests at this one, that she added some words of her own, the only time she did so in speaking of the apparitions. 'A chapel – as quickly as possible, even if it's very small.'

She could not even be sure, when questioned, if the lady had said the procession was to be on Thursday or any other day. No, she did not know the lady's name, or who she might be.

'Then you must ask her to tell you her name,' Dean Peyramale ordered.

He allowed the other priests to take up the questioning. A query from her own confessor, Fr Pomian, concerned the rumour that Bernadette had blessed rosaries and other pious objects at the grotto. She explained that people often asked her, at the grotto and elsewhere, to bless or even to touch things; this annoyed her, and her reply always was, 'I don't wear a stole, do I? That's for the priest to do.' This was to be her consistent attitude to all such requests for the rest of her life. The report about the rosaries at the grotto, no doubt brought to the ears of the clergy by some pious busybody, arose from the misinterpretation of one of Bernadette's actions during an ecstasy. When, at one point, she happened to lift her hand carrying her rosary beads towards the grotto, many people in the crowd raised their own beads in an imitative gesture of devotion.

Thinking perhaps of peasant folklore, one of the priests puzzled Bernadette with questions about witches and fairies until the literate and experienced Dominiquette – she had often travelled to other areas on her brother's coaches – pointed out to them that Bernadette did not understand the terms they were using since they were not the names of those things in Bernadette's local dialect.

The presence of the other priests and of Mlle Cazenave caused Dean Peyramale to behave with more courtesy, but with no less firmness, when bidding his visitors goodbye. His respite was short-lived.

On the evening of the next day, after another apparition at which 3,000 people saw Bernadette in ecstasy, she was back at his door.

'Well,' he greeted her, less sternly this time, 'did you ask her name?'

Bernadette had done so, several times.

'And what did she say?'

'She only smiled.'

'Ah! She's having fun with you,' he told her.

'But she still wants the chapel,' Bernadette said bravely.

The priest considered for a while. Then, recalling the 16th century apparition of Our Lady to the peasant, Juan Diego, at Guadalupe in Mexico, he decided to challenge Bernadette's Aquerò by asking for a sign (when Juan came to the local bishop, a Spaniard, with the Lady's request for a chapel, the bishop asked for a miraculous sign and was convinced when Juan returned later with roses in his cloak which he had gathered, at the Lady's direction, on the bleak mountain-top in mid-winter – the image of the apparition was imprinted on the cloak).

'So, the lady wants a chapel?' said Dean Peyramale. 'Well then, if she really wants this chapel, first let her tell you her name, and then – you know that rosebush in the grotto at Massabielle? – tell her to make that rosebush blossom now, in this month of March. Then we'll build a chapel there.' He added, warming to his theme, 'and you can tell her it won't be a small one, like you said; no, it will be a fine big one!'

Bernadette meekly promised to convey his terms to the beautiful lady at the grotto and then went back home to take up once again, as she always did after any vision, interrogation or other encounter, the daily routine of her simple and happy life in the bosom of her loving family.

CHAPTER ELEVEN

Great Expectations

Thursday 4 March 1858 was the last of the fifteen days on which Bernadette had been asked by the lady to come to the grotto. The belief had grown stronger with every passing day that something of great significance would happen at this last appearance of the lady whom Bernadette was still calling simply Aquerò. As with the reports of miracles, Bernadette had never said anything to that effect. However, the police authorities still feared trouble, one way or the other, when such a huge and excitable crowd gathered at Massabielle. Police Commissioner Jacomet was meticulous in his precautionary measures. Police were drafted in from other areas to help quell any disturbance that might ensue either from the expected great revelation or from frustration at the lack of it. Jacomet took charge in person. He went to the grotto at 11 pm the night before and inspected the whole area, including the grotto itself in the cliff face to which access, albeit difficult, was possible from a narrow passage at the rear. He assured himself that no machines or fireworks or other material helps to a fake miracle were in place; he also noted, with some surprise, that the lanterns and candles of people praying were already illuminating the area around the cavern and the grotto.

By the time Jacomet and his men returned at 5 am for another inspection, they found it difficult to make their way through the now much larger crowds which included people from other towns and valleys as well as many soldiers from the fort. Again, Jacomet was surprised at the calm and devout atmosphere, the unusually polite and helpful behaviour in such a mob. By 7 am, the time at which Bernadette usually arrived on the most recent occasions, so huge was the crowd around that dark cliff at Massabielle that estimates vary wildly between 8,000 and 20,000. Other people besides Jacomet had taken preparatory measures. Unlike that first day when she had hesitated to take off her shoes and stockings in order to follow her sister and their friend through the icy water of the stream, on this auspicious day Bernadette was able to gain access to the grotto across a footbridge of planks laid down that evening by a local wheelwright; other local men helped the police in guiding and marshalling the ever-increasing crowds coming from all directions.

When Bernadette knelt in her usual place below the niche in the cliff, her cousin, Jeanne Védère, a 30-year-old teacher from Momère, knelt beside her – she had asked that favour of Bernadette. They had attended Mass in the town at 6.30 am and then walked to the grotto. At the second decade of the rosary, Bernadette went into ecstasy, watched by the huge but hushed crowd who imitated her each time she devoutly made the Sign of the Cross. Commissioner Jacomet was an exception – he and the Deputy Mayor were too busy observing and noting down every move and gesture of the ecstatic young girl. Jacomet noted meticulously that she made 34 smiles and 24 bows in the direction of the grotto.

After about half an hour, Bernadette rose from her knees and went in under the sloping roof of the cavern to the point where she usually held her conversations with the apparition. The people near her could see her lips moving and her happy smiling face, but no sound was heard by anyone in the hushed thousands around her. She remained near the niche for about two minutes, during which, as Jeanne Védère later testified, she smiled very often but grew sad now and again. Then she bowed towards the apparition and went back to kneel again and resume her recitation of the rosary for almost fifteen minutes more. Altogether, this apparition was one of the longest in the series, lasting by Jacomet's official timing, from 7.15 am to 8 am. Then, without saying a word to anyone, Bernadette rose, quenched her candle, and made her way through the silent, respectful thousands thronged around the grotto. She headed in the direction of the town. There had been no great miracle or message. The big day was just like many of the other fifteen days, albeit not as disappointing as the two days on which there had been no apparition.

The most relieved man in France on that March morning was possibly Commissioner Domenique Jacomet of Lourdes. He and his men were prepared for two developments, either that Bernadette, coming out of her ecstasy, would face the people and make some announcement of a forthcoming wonder or natural disaster, or that, if no such announcement were forthcoming, the disappointment and frustration of the thousands gathered there would erupt into a riot. Neither happened. Even while the Soubirous girl was calmly walking away in silence, the crowd began to disperse quietly, apart from those who stayed kneeling in prayer or others who went to drink or wash or fill bottles and other containers at the spring. Jacomet's report would be more than welcome to his superiors. His handling of the whole affair, especially on this last and potentially dangerous day, would be another feather in his policeman's hat.

His clerical counterpart, Dean Peyramale, was not present at the apparition. He waited anxiously, probably in prayer, for the visit that he felt sure would come. So it did, albeit belatedly. Bernadette, on returning home with her family, found crowds of people gathering at their door. They wanted to see and embrace her, to beg her to touch their rosaries and medals, even to offer her money and other gifts. When someone tried to slip a gold coin into her hands, she rejected it vigorously and cried, 'No, no, it burns me!' Fortunately for Bernadette, all appeals to bless things were met with her standard rebuttal, all gifts and money refused sternly. Among those who offered money there were agents of Jacomet, including a policeman and some civilians, the latter including the wife of Sergeant D'Angla. Other visitors included a group of three doctors who had decided to question Bernadette. The family finally succeeded in closing their door in order to eat their midday meal. Bernadette took advantage of the lull in callers to visit the Parish Priest.

If Commissioner Jacomet was a relieved man that day because nothing had happened and there was no message, Dean Peyramale was disappointed for the same reason. Bernadette had no news for him, except that when she asked the lady's name again, the lady just smiled. The same serene smile was the only reply to the priest's challenge to make the old rosebush at the grotto bloom out of season.

'But she still wants the chapel,' Bernadette concluded.

'Does she?' he responded, with a touch of his former sarcasm, 'and do you have the money to build this chapel?' He knew the futility of such a question.

'No, Reverend Father,' Bernadette admitted humbly.

'Well, neither do I,' he snapped, 'so, go and tell the lady to give it to you.'

Like Jacomet, Dean Peyramale would continue his reports to his superior, in this case the bishop, including the repeated demand for a chapel and the increasing number of cures being claimed as a result of combining the water at the grotto with prayer to Our Blessed Lady, now identified by believers in the apparitions, except Bernadette herself, as the lady in the grotto; but he was still in an invidious position, unable to approve or disapprove, and fully aware of what would be made by the anticlerical scoffers of the non-event at the grotto this very day.

From the priest's house, Bernadette went to the house of Antoine Clarens, the headmaster who had visited the grotto in order to write an account for the provincial Prefect but who had since invited her to stay at his house if ever she needed to rest or to escape from the attention of the public. He reported afterwards his amazement on this occasion at seeing how Bernadette joined so naturally in the play of his own children, seeming to forget all the disputes and notoriety that were her daily lot. Her stay was short that day.

Back at her own poor home, the crowds had gathered again, and among them the doctors who wanted to continue their much interrupted interview of the morning. In the afternoon, François Soubirous came to the headmaster's house to collect his daughter. The crowds around his door, especially those who had come from distant villages and towns, would not go away until they had seen the young girl whom many now regarded so favoured by heaven that she must be a saint. Bernadette's father was offered some free professional advice by one of the three doctors who examined Bernadette that day. 'If you want your children to survive,' the medical visitor said, 'you should move them from this foul hovel of a place.' Like most such well-wishers, he did not himself offer a more salubrious alternative.

Now that the period of the apparitions had ended, as Bernadette and the public believed, the Soubirous family hoped to resume their former peaceful if penurious way of life. The anti-clerical press, both in Lourdes and elsewhere, also mockingly assumed that the non-event on the 'big day' of 4 March brought down the final curtain on the farce at Massabielle. The local paper, *Lavédan*, was condescending in its verdict: 'What a disappointment! How these poor credulous people have been humiliated! How many of them have realised, all too late unfortunately, the ridiculousness of their behaviour and regretted their excessive credulity!' Another editor was more severe: 'The real miracle is the amazing credulousness of this throng, who have not been undeceived even by their own disappointment.' While the Prefect's own official organ, *L'Ere Impériale*, concluded its denigratory report and analysis with a recommendation: 'This whole affair could have been cut short if the alleged saint of eleven had been sent to the local hospice as an unbalanced person.' The alleged saint was, of course, fourteen, but such details do not bother the concentrated mind of the prejudiced.

Such reports, avidly read and discussed by the readers of those newspapers, did not bother Bernadette. Being still illiterate, newspapers formed no part of her life. She was not even aware that the national press of France was beginning to hear about events at Lourdes and to mention 'the young visionary,' or that the Catholic press, as prudently cautious up to this as the clergy had been, was also taking up the story. The main concern of the 'young visionary' at this time was to be allowed to receive her First Holy Communion, which she hoped to do as soon as the nuns at the hospice school assured the Parish Priest that she knew enough Christian doctrine to be allowed so great a privilege.

The expectation of a peaceful return to normal life was shattered when Bernadette was once again brought before the Police Commissioner and other official interrogators, a fortnight after what she and they had assumed to be the end of the apparitions. The relief of the Commissioner and his superiors had been shaken by the fact that crowds were continuing to go to the grotto, both to pray at what was now regarded as a shrine, and to wash in the water of the spring and take away containers of the water. On the day the water first began to flow, two local men dug a channel for it; later they used clods of turf to fashion a crude basin. Then a local tinsmith replaced this with a zinc basin that had three spigots – the first version of what is today the row of taps nearby. A carpenter designed a board to hold the candles people wanted to leave lighting at the grotto and, to make access easier, local quarrymen cut out trails and steps in the steep slope that led to the grotto from behind Massabielle, the slope down which Mme Milhet had made an undignified descent on the day of the third apparition. Perhaps because the request about a procession was now common knowledge, the people did not wait for the clergy to fulfil that request of the lady of the grotto; they were already coming in organised groups, much like spontaneous processions, with hymns, candles and prayers at the grotto. The guilds of Lourdes had decided to supervise and direct all this activity at the grotto.

Reporting these developments, as well as the gifts people were leaving in the crevices all around the grotto – not only money and small statues, but strange items like a veil and a lump of cheese – the puzzled Sergeant D'Angla was careful to note that nobody asked remuneration for any work done in connection with the grotto; stranger still, while money and gifts were brought – one poor woman was seen to leave a gold piece, reminding people of the widow observed by Jesus furtively putting her small life savings in the temple fund – nothing was being stolen.

The reaction of Commisioner Jacomet and the other officials to these developments was that, in spite of the fact that the apparitions had ended, there must still be something going on that they had not discovered. Although reports from the Sergeant and others made it clear that Bernadette had not been seen at the grotto since the 'big day' on 4 March, the authorities decided that she should be questioned about these undesirable developments. They subjected Bernadette to another four hours of interrogation, going over the same questions and getting the same unshakeable replies. A new topic was the reported miracles and what her personal connection with them. Was she claiming now that she was a healer?

'I know nothing about miracles,' Bernadette protested. 'I do not believe that I have cured anyone. I have done nothing to that purpose.'

Questioned about the continuing devotions at the grotto, she maintained that it had nothing to do with her; if people went there to pray, that was their own business. For herself, she said, 'I don't know if I will go back to the grotto any more.'

The Commissioner was satisfied, at least as far as this troublesome Soubirous child was concerned as a potential source of public unrest. In his report he made his policeman's interpretation of her statements. 'She does not seem to want to tangle with the local authorities.'

CHAPTER TWELVE

The Real Big Day

The Feast of the Annunciation, 25 March, is one of the great days dedicated to the honour of the Blessed Virgin Mary. It commemorates the greatest event in the history of the human race, an event narrated by the evangelist Luke thus: 'In the sixth month the Angel Gabriel was sent by God to a town in Galilee called Nazareth, to a virgin betrothed to a man named Joseph, of the House of David; and the virgin's name was Mary. He went in and said to her: "Rejoice, you who enjoy God's favour! The Lord is with you." She was deeply disturbed by these words and asked herself what this greeting could mean, but the angel said to her, "Mary, do not be afraid; you have won God's favour. Look! You are to conceive in your womb and bear a son, and you must name him Jesus. He will be great and will be called Son of the Most High".'

As if the Angel Gabriel was now being sent to another young girl chosen by God for a special purpose, it was on the day when the whole church celebrates the Annunciation to Mary that Bernadette was awakened from her sleep by a new urge to go to the grotto. She did not know that her beautiful and beloved Aquerò, whom she thought she would not see again, and who had just smiled silently on all the occasions when Bernadette conveyed the query of the Parish Prist as to her identity, had herself chosen the day on which she would answer that question.

In spite of her parents' protests, Bernadette set out for the grotto at 5 am. As usual, word spread rapidly – because of the day that was in it, there were people praying at the candlelit grotto even through the night, observed by one or other of Jacomet's agents – and when Bernadette began her rosary she was surrounded by family and friends and hundreds of other onlookers. When she went into ecstasy, the crowd saw her rise and approach near to the cavity as she always did when entering into conversation with the apparition. They did not know that in the course of that conversation, Bernadette, this time of her own accord and making no mention of demands from the Parish Priest, asked the lady to tell her name. Having bowed politely, she said, as she later reported, 'Mademoiselle, would you be so kind as to tell me who you are, if you please?' The result at first was as before, Aquerò smiled silently. This time, Bernadette persisted, remembering that the priest had made identification of the apparition a condition for the building of a chapel at the grotto. As if testing the young girl's faith, a second and a third polite request met with the same smiling silence. When Bernadette persisted, with another bow and another request, the joined hands of Aquerò opened out and extended towards the ground as if taking in the whole world; then she joined her hands again, raised her eyes to the sky, and spoke words in the *patois* which was Bernadette's own language. She said: *Que soy era Immaculada Councepciou.*

At last, at last, the beautiful young lady had given herself a name! But the feeling of joy and relief that flooded Bernadette's soul did not have any effect on her mind and understanding. She did not know what this strange name meant; nevertheless, it was a name, an answer for the Parish Priest, and it might be something that he would understand and be satisfied with. The watching people saw her return to her normal state, turn quickly and rush away towards the town, her lips moving all the time. She was repeating the strange name to herself lest she forget it on the way.

Before Dean Peyramale had time to greet her, whether with sarcasm or kindness, she joyfully spoke the words she had memorised: *Que soy era Immaculada Councepciou.*

The priest could not have been more shocked if an angel or a devil had appeared on the floor of his house. This girl was actually saying: I am the Immaculate Conception. He knew what those words meant; he knew also that this illiterate girl did not, but that she was certainly not claiming to make that statement about herself. While he tried to recover from shock, his mind began to analyse the portentous words she had uttered in her innocence; they did not constitute a name, but rather a theological declaration. Only four years earlier, another declaration had been made that used those same words, Immaculate Conception. Pope Pius IX in Rome, head of the Catholic Church, Vicar of Christ on earth, infallible teacher of the faithful in matters of doctrine, had declared as a dogma of the church, to be believed by all, that the Blessed Virgin Mary was conceived free, by God's grace, from the common human stain and handicap termed in theology Original Sin. The Parish Priest of Lourdes knew only too well that many Catholics did not comprehend the theology involved in that papal pronouncement. Even if this young girl in his own parish had ever heard any reference to the new dogma, it would have been in French, a language she knew little of; in any language, it would have passed over her innocent head.

Dean Peyramale, from initially regarding the report of apparitions as suspect, had been torn between doubt and belief according as the number of believers increased and the evidence of good religious results became apparent. He had also, personally and through his curates and other reliable contacts, learned much more about the young girl who was claiming to see visions at Massabielle. He was in no doubt by now of her innocence and truthfulness. He knew that even after several gruelling interrogations, the police and other authorities had been unable to find the least evidence of involvement or manipulation by her relatives or by any pious plotters. He was now standing before a child, as he considered her, who was actually claiming, without knowing it herself, that the Blessed Virgin Mary, Mother of God, had appeared and spoken to her over and over again. His own soul was shaken to the extent that, as he later related, he almost broke down in tears. Yet, he felt that he should reassure himself.

'You must be mistaken!' he told Bernadette. 'That's not a name, a woman could not have that for a name. Do you know what it means?'

'No, Reverend Father,' she replied humbly – and truthfully, as he well knew.

'Then how can you say such words if you don't even know what they mean?'

'I kept saying them all the way as I came here.' She had something to add, even if it might cause him to shout at her as he had done before. 'She still wants the chapel.' The child was as much as saying: 'I got you a name, just like you asked.' And it was now up to him, the Parish Priest, to fulfil his promise!

He was too moved in his own soul to be able to do more than order her firmly to go back home. 'I'll see you another time,' he said.

Bernadette left him to his worries. With her peasant dependance on memory, she was now quite sure of the words she had repeated so often, the strange name Aquerò had given herself. It did not worry her that she did not understand it, or that he had not explained it to her. She had told the Priest and that was her job done. Later she visited the young tax official, Jean-Baptiste Estrade, and his sister, Emmanuelite, who were devout believers in her visions and always eager to hear her speak about them. When she asked them to explain the strange name the lady had given herself, they realised, like the Parish Priest, that Bernadette herself did not comprehend the privilege heaven had bestowed on her. They told her, 'It's the Blessed Virgin Mary you have been seeing.' It was what some people had been surmising from the first apparition, what more began to believe as time went on, and what the increasing crowds coming to pray at the grotto now firmly believed. Estrade and his sister would have appreciated, as Dean Peyramale did, not only this heavenly confirmation of the papal pronouncement four years earlier, but the significance of the fact that the Lady of the grotto had chosen this day, the Feast of the Annunciation to her by the Angel

Gabriel, to make her own annunciation to the young girl God had chosen as its innocent recipient.

Bernadette could now appreciate with even greater happiness the manner in which the Lady of the grotto smiled at her when she recited the rosary – and why the Lady herself fingered her own beautiful beads but never moved her lips while doing so. In the humility of her innocent soul, Bernadette must have wondered why such a wonderful thing had happened to her, a poor, ignorant girl as she saw herself. She cannot have realised that from that very day, as the news of what she had told her Parish Priest spread like wildfire, first throughout Lourdes itself, increasingly through France and the whole Catholic world, her life could never be the same again.

CHAPTER THIRTEEN

The Last Apparitions

A few days later, Bernadette was again examined by the three doctors who had visited her previously at the *cachot*; they were now instructed by the authorities to seek the evidence of mental affliction that would justify her being put away in an institution. Her confessor, Fr Pomian, laughed when he heard of this, stating that they would not find anywhere a mind so healthy and sane as that of Bernadette. They reported in diplomatic and contradictory terms: they found no indication of mental ill-health, but they considered that Bernadette was a troubled child who would, if people stopped bothering her and asking for her prayers, resume her ordinary life and stop seeing things at the grotto and talking about marvellous things, as she had been doing.

On the same day, Commissioner Jacomet was reporting to his superiors that the business at the grotto was getting even worse. As Easter approached, the crowds of pilgrims increased, and they were coming from farther afield, even some from Paris. Bouquets, money, all sorts of things were being left at the grotto, and that spring water the girl had found was still gushing strongly and being taken away not only all over the Lourdes area but all over France. Jacomet's men thought they had apprehended thieves when they saw some local men, whom they knew to be in poor circumstances, gathering up the money left at the grotto – they were amazed to find that this was being done on a regular and organised basis, the money being brought to Dean Peyramale as a collective donation for Masses from the pilgrims. The good Dean of Lourdes, a poor parish, was glad of what could literally be considered a godsend, but not, as will be seen later, for personal reasons.

98

On Easter Monday, 5 April, Bernadette received an invitation from Blaise Vergès, ex-mayor of the town of Adé, four kilometres from Lourdes. His reported cure at the grotto was causing a lot of public comment and was a cause of further frustration for Jacomet – bad enough that the credulous common people were claiming to be cured, but here was one of the upper class, a former mayor, telling all and sundry about his personal 'miracle.' M Vergès had been suffering for years from rheumatism that had left him almost incapable; he could not dress himself without assistance and – an added agony for a devout Catholic – he could not so much as raise his hand to bless himself. He decided to visit the grotto. Accompanied by his doctor, he came, prayed, and then, undressed to the waist by his servant, painfully washed in the water from the spring as well as he could manage. Some cynics who knew him thought it a ridiculous spectacle and commented that old Vergès would soon be cured of his rheumatism because he would contract pneumonia and die. On the contrary, his amazed doctor confirmed some days later that he was again active and capable of using all his limbs normally. This was the distinguished man who now sent his son to invite Bernadette to dine at his home the next day, accompanied by Dean Peyramale; his son would collect them in the family carriage. Reluctant as a peasant girl like Bernadette would be to sit at table in such company, she had no option but to accept such an invitation.

When he drove her home next day, Vergès junior heard Bernadette tell her parents that she felt again a strong urge to visit the grotto. They were aghast at her announcement – now that the apparitions were at an end, as everyone believed, they had begun to feel secure from any further trouble. If Bernadette began going to the grotto again, huge crowds would follow her; this would bring Jacomet and his minions pounding on the door of the *cachot* again to arrest their daughter and perhaps themselves as well. Young Vergès had a solution: he would drive Bernadette back to his father's house where she would be welcome to stay the night; very early next morning he would drive her back to Lourdes by way of Massabielle; thus she would be able to visit the grotto without drawing public attention. Little did he know how closely every movement of the Soubirous family, especially of Bernadette herself, was instant news both for the police and for the public. When Bernadette arrived at the grotto at around 7 am next morning, over a thousand people had already gathered there, their candles lit, their rosaries in their hands, while more were arriving from all directions. Jacomet's men were also in place, ready to note down all that happened. On that day, there would be something unusual to add to their routine reports of praying and ecstasy.

Among those who had been alerted by the grapevine was Dr Duzous, one of the anti-clerical freethinkers of Lourdes who had visited the grotto in February with the stated object of observing Bernadette and making a scientific report that would silence all talk of supernatural influence on her physical and mental condition. He had indeed observed her with all his professional acumen, and had expressed his amazement at the transformation in her features and attitude; but he had been unable to come to a diagnosis that would serve his preconceived verdict. The more he and his fellow-intellectuals discussed the happenings at Massabielle, the more he became less sure of his materialistic interpretation of them.

Perhaps because he was wary of further emotional impressions, or was deterred by the dismissive cynicism of others, Dr Duzous had not repeated his visit to the grotto. He may have come to regret this, now that the apparitions seemed to be at an end. This might explain why, on being roused from sleep by some friend early on this Easter Wednesday, 7 April, with the news that the girl had gone to the grotto again, he dressed hurriedly and ran to the grotto, arriving there red-faced and panting to find a large crowd already on their knees and Bernadette already in ecstasy.

In his personal testimony later, he wryly admitted that some of the devout people present manifested their annoyance at the fact that he did not remove his hat; he had to explain to them, as a medical man, that he was perspiring so much that he feared he might catch cold! When that whispered contention died down, the crowd deferred to his professional status and allowed him access to the front rank where he could observe Bernadette very closely.

The Vergès family at Adé had provided Bernadette with a larger than usual candle, the kind carried in processions. This was too heavy to hold in her hands, especially while praying her rosary; so, she had stood it on the ground. Now Dr Duzous saw, along with the other people watching, that Bernadette had cupped her hands around the flame of the candle to protect it from the gentle breeze. To their amazement and horror, however, they also saw that, because she was in ecstasy, she was unaware that her hands were actually in contact with the flame! Some cried out in alarm, 'She's burning!' and moved to protect the unconscious girl from harm; but Dr Duzous restrained them. 'Wait! Let her be!' He had observed that, although the flame of the candle was in contact with her two hands, those hands did not move. Fascinated, but still aware of his scientific intent, he took out his watch and counted the minutes. For almost fifteen minutes, while every gust of wind blew the flame of the candle even more against her hands, Bernadette went on praying silently, gazing in rapture towards the opening in the cliff face. Then she came out of her ecstasy as usual.

Rushing forward, Dr Duzous grabbed her two hands and examined them closely. There was no sign of a burn or any damage to the skin. He cried out to the people gathered around, 'No burns! Nothing!' Then he suddenly moved one of the girl's hands back to the still lighting candle. As soon as the flame touched her skin, Bernadette cried out, 'Oh, you're hurting me!' The flame of atheism died in the soul of Dr Duzous while Bernadette was blowing out the flame of the Vergès candle. He fell on his knees and turned his face to the cave of the apparitions. Later that day, in the Café français, he related the prodigious event to the company. With the enthusiasm of a new believer added to his natural exuberance, Dr Duzous even went and told Police Commissioner Jacomet who, ever the meticulous policeman, duly noted and reported what could not have been welcome news to him, a detailed factual account from an educated professional man who had hitherto been as sceptical as his colleagues and who was now proclaiming another 'miracle' all over the town. Dr Duzous even used the word supernatural: 'For me, it was supernatural to see Bernadette on her knees before the grotto, in ecstasy, holding a lighted candle and covering the flames with her two hands, without her seeming to have the least impression of her hands' contact with the flame. I examined her hands. Not the slightest trace of burns.'

Laying down his pen after finishing that report, Jacomet probably sighed and thought, 'Where is all this nonsense going to end if even a doctor is seeing things now?'

Another kind of nonsense was just beginning. All kinds of apparitions and visions were being seen, some more fantastic than others. There were even hints of a diabolic interest in the grotto of Massabielle in some of the grotesque distortions and grimaces with which some of the self-styled visionaries tried to imitate what had been reported about Bernadette in ecstasy. At the grotto itself, a few days after the apparition at which Dr Duzous saw what he was now calling the miracle of the candle, five women, having procured a ladder from a nearby farm, climbed to an opening in the rock from which, through a narrow passage, they made their way by the light of candles into a dark area behind the niche in which Bernadette had seen Our Lady. They came out claiming that they had seen a vision of a lady in white. They even went to Dean Peyramale with this news. The Parish Priest, more inclined now to listen to such stories, received them quietly and took note of their 'vision', which, on being subjected to police investigation by Jacomet, turned out to be a white stalactite in the dark cave. The epidemic of visions and visionaries became so widespread during the ensuing months that the bishop had to issue a letter denouncing all such incidents; upon which, to the surprise even of Jacomet, they dwindled and ceased.

Meanwhile, the provincial Prefect had issued a proclamation on 4 May which declared: 'Any person claiming to see visions will be immediately arrested and brought to the hospital in Tarbes.' If he had hoped to include Bernadette in this ultimatum, she was not to be found in Lourdes. By now, Bernadette was no longer the poor defenceless Soubirous girl, daughter of that disreputable ex-miller who had done some time in jail for theft. She had friends and protectors in all ranks of society – there was even an elderly retired judge who incurred official disapproval because he advised her about the traps that might be laid by her interrogators. Perhaps as a result of a warning from that or some other source, Bernadette had been taken away from Lourdes to Cauterets where, incidentally, it was hoped her asthma might be relieved. Even there, however, she was pestered by people wanting to touch her or asking her to bless objects of piety. To all such she gave the answer she had given to the people in Lourdes, 'I'm not a priest, I can't bless anything.' She added, 'If you believe in God, go and pray.' She also, as reported to Jacomet by the local police commissioner, continued vigorously to reject all offers of money or gifts.

On returning home, Bernadette resumed attendance at the hospice school, and on 3 June she at last had the great happiness of receiving her First Holy Communion. She had not reached the standard in knowledge of the catechism required by the theological lawmakers in such matters; but as her confessor, Fr Pomian, pointed out, who would dare to say that a child who had been so favoured by heaven was to be denied the privilege of receiving Holy Communion just because she could not memorise the catechism? Bernadette herself had commented, as she had done some years previously at Bartrès when her former nurse made a few attempts to instruct her, that they might as well try to put the book into her head as get her to learn all those big words off by heart. Some of Bernadette's biographers have remarked on the analogy with St John Vianney, Curé of Ars (1786-1859) who was ordained priest in spite of his inability to become proficient in Latin and was to become the most sought-after confessor and spiritual counsellor in France (he died just one year after the apparitions at Lourdes). Inevitably, Bernadette was asked, 'Which made you happier, your First Communion or the apparitions?' As with all such queries, whether sincere or from ulterior motives, her answer had the depth and simplicity of inspiration. 'The two things go together, but they cannot be compared. I was very happy with both.'

In the meantime, the authorities had decided that the only way to put an end to the gatherings and devotions at the grotto was to make it illegal to go there. All the objects left there were removed and wooden barricades were erected with notices declaring the area to be out of bounds. Among those who protested against this probibition was Dr Duzous, who based his protest not only on religious but on medical grounds – if sick or handicapped people were obtaining cures or even solace by using the water of the grotto in conjunction with prayer, why should they be prevented from going to the grotto, especially as there was no evidence of any public disorder or criminal activity? He collected over three hundred signatures to a petition against the closure of the grotto.

Also uneasy about the ban was Mayor Lacadé, the man who had eagerly welcomed one of the first, but mistaken, chemical analyses of the water at the grotto as having medicinal qualities. Although disappointed in their hopes of a lucrative spa at Lourdes when it was shown by expert analysis that it was just ordinary water, Mayor Lacadé and the business people of Lourdes were now having visions of their own, visions that had no connection with supernatural manifestations. They were taking note of the increase in visitors, even from Paris itself, coming to inquire about the Soubirous girl and to visit the grotto. Constable Callet, whose guard duty at the barricaded grotto included noting the names and addresses of all who defied the Prefect's ban on visitors, had recently recorded, in his faulty spelling, the names of a high-class group from Paris: an admiral's widow, governess of the imperial prince, with her two children, accompanied by a priest and a nun. They had spoken with

Bernadette at her home. Later, having prayed on their knees at the wooden barricade, the lady asked the embarrassed Constable Callet if he would be so kind as to fill a carafe with water from the spring, and also to fetch for her some small stones and clods of earth from the area of the grotto. The poor fellow did so, under cover of fulfilling one of his other duties, that of collecting the bouquets, candles, etc. left at the grotto and throwing them into the river. He refused the money offered by the party; but they later left it at his own home.

Mayor Lacadé and the town council were aware that enterprising hawkers, as well as some local inns, had already begun to sell candles, medals, small statues and bouquets – even empty bottles! – to visitors who came from distant towns and cities to visit the grotto. If this went on, there would soon be need of new hotels, restaurants, souvenir shops, etc. And when the promised railway came to Lourdes – the increasing hordes of pilgrims would hasten that development – perhaps that very ordinary water dug up by Bernadette at Massabielle would prove even more profitable for the town than any spa, and the grotto could turn out to be an inexhaustible gold mine.

The Mayor and his business friends probably noted with satisfaction that as soon as Jacomet's wooden barricades were erected, they were pulled down at night and thrown in the river Gave. This went on for some time until finally, in October, the authorities gave up – some said it was by order from Paris of the Emperor himself – and the grotto became legally accessible again. In the meantime, Bernadette had seen the final vision of the Lady whose identity she now knew. Again, as on the day when the Lady finally made known who she was, it seemed as if the day for this last apparition was chosen significantly by Our Lady herself.

16 July is the date of another Feast Day of Our Lady, that of Our Lady of Mount Carmel. On that day, Bernadette once more felt the irresistible urge to go to the grotto; but it was now proclaimed out of bounds and the barricade made it impossible of access. Bernadette adapted her course to these circumstances.

She waited until late in the evening, and then, wearing a dark hood instead of the usual white one which had become so recognisable, she went with her Aunt Lucile and a few others to the meadow on the opposite side of the River Gave from Massabielle. There were other groups of people there, praying by the light of their candles. Bernadette knelt and lit her own candle. As soon as she began to recite the rosary, her face lit up with joy. She opened her hands and gazed in ecstasy towards the grotto on the far side of the river. Her lips did not move and she seemed to hear no voice. This final apparition, like some of the earlier ones, was a vision without conversation. When it ended, Bernadette rose and walked away quietly. On the way, she said: 'I saw neither the boards nor the Gave. It seemed to me that I was in the grotto, no more distant than the other times. I saw only the Holy Virgin.'

It was the end of the apparitions. It was also a new beginning in the life of the innocent and humble young girl who had been chosen by heaven to see those apparitions and to convey the message of prayer and penance from the Blessed Virgin Mary to the human race.

CHAPTER FOURTEEN

After the Apparitions

Bernadette was to live for twenty-one years more. Those years fall into two distinct periods. Having lived with her parents for two years after the apparitions, two years during which she was constantly sought out by visitors of all kinds and social classes, in July 1860 she was taken in as a boarder at the hospice of the Sisters of Charity of Nevers at Lourdes, where she had been for some time a pupil in the class for poor children. She remained in the hospice for six years, still being subjected to interviews and visits, until in July 1866, at the age of 22, she achieved her long-formed desire to become a Sister of Charity herself. She entered the convent at Nevers and lived there until her death on 16 April 1879.

In the two years she spent with her family after the apparitions, Bernadette tried to resume her previous way of life. In addition to helping in their poor home, she went out to earn some money for the family as a nurse-maid. She also tried to catch up on the lessons she had missed through her recurring bouts of asthma and other illnesses by availing of lessons offered by friends. Her name and story were now in the national press, largely as a result of the visit of Louis Veuillot, Parisian editor of *L'Univers*, the leading Catholic paper, who interviewed her on the same day as Madame Brouat and her party, and duly had his name entered in the notebook of Constable Callet. The famous journalist voiced his indignation: 'And so they actually want to prevent people from praying to the good God here!' He interviewed Bernadette before a large audience in the shop of M Pailhasson, a pharmacist, with Fr Pomian as interpreter between the *patois* of Bernadette and the standard French of M Veuillot.

After she left, he remarked, 'She's illiterate – but she's worth more than anyone like me.' His interview with Bernadette filled five columns in *L'Univers* and would have been read by the highest ecclesiastical authorities in France as well as by Catholics generally. From such a source, the story was picked up even by the anti-Catholic press.

Although Bernadette herself never went to the grotto now, and avoided all voluntary reference to the apparitions – to all who spoke to her about miracles, she replied that she personally knew nothing about them – the problems resulting from the apparitions for herself and her family increased to the point where they had a constant stream of people coming to their door, wanting to speak to Bernadette and offering objects of piety for her to touch. She rejected all such requests as before, as she sternly refused any offers of money – her young brother told later how she gave him a box on the ear and made him return a gold piece he was given by some wealthy people who sent him to fill a bottle at the grotto. She could not, of course, refuse whenever Dean Peyramale or the Mayor sent for her to meet distinguished visitors at the priest's house or at the hotel. Some were learned priests who tried out their theological tricks in vain on this peasant girl. Like others of their kind later, they were especially interested in the three secrets Bernadette said she had been told by the Blessed Virgin Mary, secrets that were for herself alone and that she never divulged. Other questioners were less interested in theology than in sensationalism, like the enterprising journalist who offered to take her to Paris and make her famous and rich.

Bishop Thibault of Montpellier, who interviewed her at the parochial house only a day after the last apparition, tried to coax her to swap her rosary beads for his own beautiful beads – blessed, he told her, by the Pope himself. 'Thank you, Reverend Father', she protested – she did not know he was a bishop – 'but I prefer my own rosary.'

A few days later Bernadette was sent for again. Another bishop had arrived in Lourdes. Bishop Cardon de Garsignies of

Soissons got the same impression as the other man, that he was dealing with a truthful and saintly young girl. They both wrote to the local bishop, urging him to set up an episcopal commission of inquiry into the apparitions. While officially staying aloof and ordering his clergy to do likewise, Bishop Laurence of Tarbes had kept himself well informed, from Dean Peyramale and other sources, about all the happenings at Lourdes since the first report of an apparition on 11 February. He was now willing to make an official inquiry into the matter. He formally set up a commission to do so. This would mean that as the interrogations by the civic authorities ceased, Bernadette would have to face similar ordeals conducted by church experts in canon law. On 17 November 1858 she was summoned to the first of these, conducted by a panel of four theologians. Like everyone else who interviewed her, they were deeply impressed by her simplicity and candour, although she was uncertain now about the request for a procession – the violent rejection by Dean Peyramale had frightened her to that extent; about the request for a chapel, however, she was quite assured in her memory.

Although many visitors to the cold and dismal old dungeon that was the home of the Soubirous family, including the genteel admiral's widow and the zealous editor of *L'Univers*, had been appalled by what one visitor called 'a foul and squalid hovel', no one seems to have suggested a practical improvement of their domestic condition; if any such offers were made, it is possible that the family pride in their own dignity would have refused them. However, about two months after the end of the apparitions, in September 1858, a distant relative of the Casterot side of the family offered them a room over his café in the town. In the spring of the following year, they made another and even more salubrious move. Through the good offices of Dean Peyramale, François Soubirous was able to resume his former occupation when he was offered the tenancy of the Gras mill on the Lapaca stream. It revived his long depressed spirits, and the happy family could once again hear the sound of the rushing water and the grinding of the millstone. However, it was not long before

Louise, pregnant again, and the miller himself, fell victim once more to their innate generosity and lack of business sense. As of old, she offered hospitality to customers and visitors, while he allowed credit to the types who equate that good-natured leniency with non-payment.

The future of Bernadette was now causing concern to Dean Peyramale and others. Apart from the continuing harrassment by the faithful and by curious visitors of all kinds, the Parish Priest now thought it might be desirable to remove her from the environment at the Gras mill where the rough and bawdy conversation of the customers, as well as the possibility of improper approaches from some who had been too long in the cafés and bars of the town, were not the ideal environment for any teenage girl, let alone one whose eyes had seen the Blessed Virgin Mary herself. Already, in the summer of 1858, he had suggested to Bernadette that he might be able to arrange for her to live with the Sisters at the hospice. With her native candour, Bernadette responded: 'Oh, I know what you mean, Reverend Father, but I love my mother and father so much!' Now the priest had an ally in Mayor Lacadé who seems to have had a genuine concern for Bernadette's welfare.

Although the hospice was run by the nuns, it was funded from municipal sources as a work of charity, and the Mayor was its patron. He could arrange that Bernadette be taken in as an indigent sick girl, which of course she was, considering her asthma and racking bouts of consumptive coughing. She would not only be protected from pestering visitors and possible social dangers – Dean Peyramale still regarded her two aunts as a bad influence – but she would also have regular schooling, meals and medical attention. It was only on the promise that they could visit her, and that she could visit them – albeit accompanied by a nun – that her parents agreed to part with Bernadette. She herself was equally reluctant, but she was beginning to realise now what the Lady had meant by saying that she would not be happy in this life. Leaving her family on what was to be a permanent basis was the first sacrifice asked of her, and she offered it up in the spirit of penance that had been one of the constant messages given to her in the apparitions. Also, for some time now Bernadette had thought of becoming a nun, but her own ill-health and her conviction of unworthiness, added to the poverty that would preclude the dowry she believed essential, had served to repress the thought. Six years later, as a young woman of twenty-two, she would achieve the fulfilment of her vocation when she moved from the hospice at Lourdes to the mother house of the Sisters of Charity at Nevers.

On Sunday, 15 July 1860, Bernadette left the Gras mill and went to live as a boarder in the Lourdes hospice. One can imagine her being greeted by Mother Ursula Fardes. Only two years earlier, this same nun had expressed her attitude to the reports about visions at Massabielle by sarcastically asking the fourteen-year-old Soubirous girl, then a pupil in the poor children's First Communion class, 'Well, have you finished with your carnival fancies?' Soon a new superior, Mother Alexandrine Roques, would be happy to pose for a photographer while maternally holding the hand of that same girl standing beside her.

Although one biographer sums up the six years Bernadette spent living in the hospice at Lourdes as being spent in 'the monotonous rhythm of boarding-school life and enforced visits,' that period was marked by significant changes in Bernadette herself. In the first place, she matured from a girl of sixteen to a young woman of twenty-two. She also learned to read and write – cheerfully enduring the humiliation of having a bright ten-year-old boarder, Julie Garros, as her tutor – as well as gaining a competency in French. These intellectual advances had their drawbacks, however. The nuns ordered her to write an account of the apparitions, and also set her the task of autographing holy pictures and writing out copies of prayers in French, some of which she did not even understand. Her exposure to this formal scholastic atmosphere also caused some inhibition in her natural unaffected style of narration and a further lack of certainty about details of a story she had so often been called upon to tell by policemen, priests, distinguished visitors, and ordinary people.

Her lessons with little Julie Garros were destined to be the source of material for none other than the 'devil's advocate', the theologian charged with raising objections to a candidate's holiness, during the beatification process in 1925. The room allocated for the tuition looked out on the fruit garden of the hospice. One day, looking at the luscious strawberries outside, Bernadette's desire tussled with her conscience. Her practical mind found a solution: the boarders were forbidden to go into the garden – but not to collect strawberries. She made use of little Julie's agility: 'I'll throw my shoe out the window,' she suggested, 'and you go out and get it, and bring back some strawberries.' The devil's advocate must have been hard up for material for his brief; in any event, the holiness and sacrifices of Bernadette's life blew away that peccadillo like a wisp of straw in a gale.

It had been a condition of entering the hospice as a boarder that Bernadette would be allowed to visit her family. When she visited them at the Gras mill, in the company of Sister Victorine, she saw that her mother was pregnant and unwell – she gave birth to her second-last child, Bernard-Pierre, in September 1859 – while her father was as reckless in business as before. From other sources, she learned that her young brother and her mother had both accepted money for going to the grotto to fill bottles of water for important visitors who requested this as a special favour; also, that her aunts were now to be numbered among those who were engaged in the burgeoning business of selling religious objects to pilgrims. Bernadette must have felt that she could hardly object to her relatives doing what so many others were doing, especially as it could be said that she herself was now living in security and comparative comfort as an indirect result of the apparitions.

Further causes of penance and sacrifice were added to Bernadette's life in the hospice. She had hoped to be finished with being interviewed and displayed publicly, but the nuns summoned her to meet distinguished visitors such as bishops, and sometimes ordered her to walk in places where she could be seen by the crowds who came in hundreds, even in thousands, to try to see the visionary. She confided to a friend that she would rather suffer the periodic bouts of asthma and choking, in which she sometimes turned purple and seemed about to die, than to endure this treatment as an object of public adulation. On the other hand, the nuns themselves, and even Dean Peyramale, set themselves the task of protecting Bernadette from the danger of pride by treating her with a studied indifference that sometimes amounted to excessive humiliation. The nun with whom she used to visit home, Sister Victorine, testified later: 'I often saw her begin to cry in the doorway, when there were up to 40 or 50 people in the drawing-room waiting for her. The big tears would come, and I used to say to her, Courage! Then she would wipe away her tears, enter the room, greet everyone graciously, and try to answer all their questions. Then she would return to recreation with the other girls as if nothing had happened.'

Although obedient and self-sacrificing in all that she saw as her duty with regard to the apparitions, Bernadette retained the qualities of independence and confidence that had marked her from her earliest years. She knew her rights under the agreement she and her parents had made with the authorities, and she spoke up if she felt that her visits home or visits from her family were being curtailed. The nuns were surprised to find her with a small supply of wine from home – like the snuff she used for the relief of her asthma, it was prescribed by her doctor. The snuff was a cause of trouble one day when Bernadette offered a pinch to some of her classmates and the resultant bouts of sneezing upset the process of learning! Her friend, Sister Victorine, was puzzled on another occasion when, passing by Bernadette and her sister, Toinette, as they conferred near a window, she overheard Bernadette say: 'Don't ever learn to read.'

Later, Bernadette replied to her kind query by saying, 'Ah, we're from people where it's better to be like that.' She did not tell the nun that some of the boarders were reading cheap novels, often hiding them in their religious books. She had obviously become aware that literacy has its dangers as well as its benefits.

On 7 December 1860, Bernadette was summoned to Tarbes to undergo a final interrogation in connection with the episcopal inquiry set up by Bishop Laurence. This time, there were twelve members, along with the Secretary, Fr Fourcade, whose job it was to write down the questions of the theologians and the answers of the girl, Bernadette Soubirous. One of the questions was, 'Did the Holy Virgin have a halo?' Bernadette replied, 'What is a halo?' The learned theologian explained. Then she said, 'There was a soft light all around her.' Another canonist referred to the time when Bernadette ate some of the herb growing among the rocks of the cavern at Massabielle. 'The idea of making you eat some kind of herb does not seem to me to be an idea worthy of the Holy Virgin,' he observed sternly. 'Well,' said Bernadette calmly, 'we all eat salad, don't we?'

At the end of the long interrogation, Bernadette was asked to show them exactly how the Blessed Virgin stood when, on the Feast of the Annunciation, she spoke the portentous words: 'I am the Immaculate Conception.'

Berndette stood up, stretched out her arms, then joined her hands. While she stood thus, some of those present noticed that tears were running down the face of old Bishop Laurence. Afterwards, he spoke to the Vicar-General. 'Did you see that child?' he said, still showing his deep emotion. Thirteen months later, on 18 January 1862, the official episcopal result of the investigations was published in a declaration to the whole diocese: 'We judge that the Immaculate Mother of God truly appeared to the girl, Bernadette Soubirous.' The evidence cited comprised the spiritual results of the happenings at the grotto, those cures that were now being regarded as inexplicable by medical science, and the character and testimony of Bernadette herself.

While this episcopal judgement served to increase the number and fervour of pilgrims to the grotto, it also caused concern to Dean Peyramale who was now in the invidious position of spiritual guardian of a girl fast becoming the most talked-about person not only in France but in the Catholic world generally.

He knew that nothing hitherto had shaken either the simple candour or genuine humility of Bernadette, but he also knew that pride was the sin from which even the angels in heaven had not proved immune. His efforts to protect Bernadette were not helped when bishops and other such dignitaries came to him requesting that he arrange an interview with her. Nor was he pleased when the enthusiastic editor of *L'Univers*, Louis Veuillot, came for a second visit, this time bringing his two daughters to see the heaven-favoured girl whom they, like so many others now, embarrassed profoundly by treating her as if she were already canonised by Rome. Another source of annoyance for the gruff but charitable Parish Priest was the zeal of Dr Duzous in collecting reports of miracles and presenting them for scrutiny by the church authorities.

Bernadette continued to suffer chronic ill-health, and in April 1862 came so near to death – her family were called, and she was given the Sacrament of Last Anointing – that the rumour spread in the town that her recovery was a miracle. Bernadette herself discounted the story in spite of the surprise of the doctor who had asserted that she would not live till the next morning. He was even more surprised when, he having declared that her amazing recovery must be due to the medicines he had prescribed, she told him that she had not taken them. His irritated response to this was to suggest that she been exaggerating her illness.

The recent developments in the art of photography, now becoming a lucrative business as well as a rich man's hobby all over Europe and America, added a new area of sacrifice for Bernadette. The first to come asking her to pose for his camera was a priest, Fr Bernardou, professor of chemistry in the diocesan seminary. With Dean Peyramale's permission, he visited the hospice late in 1861 and annoyed Bernadette with his artistic fussiness. When he asked her to pose exactly and look as she had done during the apparitions, she objected, 'But she isn't there!' Two years later, in October 1863, she was photographed by M Billard-Perrin from the nearby town of Pau. In February 1864, a publisher from Tarbes, M Dutour, who was also a photographic enthusiast, obtained permission from Dean Peyramale to photograph Bernadette in the hospice and also at the grotto. He must have been on very good terms with Peyramale, because later that same year he again photographed Bernadette, this time at a studio in Tarbes where he brought her, with her friend and distant cousin, Jeanne Védère, the schoolteacher at Momères who had knelt beside Bernadette at the momentous apparition on 25 March. On a recent visit, with her father, to Bernadette at the hospice, Jeanne had suggested that they take Bernadette back home with them for a holiday. Dean Peyramale, himself a native of Momères, where his brother was a doctor, allowed her three days at first; then he went there himself and told her to stay as long as she wished, having ensured that his brother would care for her if necessary.

On 4 February 1864 Louise Soubirous gave birth to another son, who died in September of that same year. The death of an infant was a tragedy the Soubirous parents had already endured on a few occasions since their marriage; but a year later they suffered the loss of their son, Justin, not yet ten years old, and Bernadette's favourite sibling. He was the child the eleven-year-old Bernadette used to bring from their dungeon home to her mother for breast-feeding in the fields where Louise was toiling to earn a little money. It must have been one of the saddest days in Bernadette's young life when her father came to the hospice to tell her of that latest misfortune to strike their family.

CHAPTER FIFTEEN

A Statue and a Procession

One of the great events of Bernadette's six years at the Lourdes hospice was undoubtedly the installation in the grotto at Massabielle of the statue which has stood there ever since, inspiring devotion and piety in the souls of the millions of pilgrims who come to Lourdes every year. The statue was commissioned by the Lacour sisters of Lyon, two pious and wealthy ladies who, on seeing the small statue of Our Lady which had been placed in the grotto of the apparitions by some unknown hand, decided to have it replaced with a magnificent statue in Carrera marble. They offered what was considered the huge sum of 7,000 francs, plus expenses, to Joseph Fabisch, a sculptor already famous for similar religious works, the only condition being that the statue must represent as closely as possible the appearance of Our Lady as described by Bernadette herself.

When he came to Lourdes to meet Bernadette, he brought a paper, still extant, on which he had written twenty questions; her answers, he hoped, would form a comprehensive description on which he could base his effort. He was deeply impressed by her natural charm and personality, and like old Bishop Laurence, he was overwhelmed when he asked her how the Lady had joined her hands when she said, 'I am the Immaculate Conception.' In a letter, he wrote: 'Bernadette got up with the greatest simplicity. She joined her hands and raised her eyes to heaven. I have never seen anything more beautiful than the look of that young girl, consumptive to her fingertips ... One could not have the least doubt in the world about the signal favour that she had received.'

He showed Bernadette a portfolio of paintings and statues of

Our Lady by various artists, and then took her to Massabielle where he placed a silhouette in the grotto to judge the size and position of the statue. Two months later he sent Dean Peyramale a photo of the plaster model, about two-thirds the size of the projected statue. Bernadette was not pleased with it – the priest sent her comments to the sculptor. The finished statue arrived at the deanery on 30 March 1864. Bernadette was summoned to view it in the presence of Dean Peyramale and others. As if puzzled, or unwilling to hurt anyone's feelings, she at first said, hesitantly, 'Yes, that's it.' However, she was unable truthfully to hide her real feelings. After a moment, she shook her head and said sadly, 'No, that's not it.' How could priests or sculptor or anyone else have hoped that any statue would seem satisfactory to the eyes that had seen, over and over again, the smile of the living, gesturing Lady of the grotto? Bernadette's main objection was to the artistic touches, such as folds in the veil and dress, introduced by the sculptor to the detriment of the simplicity and youthfulness she always attributed to the Lady of the apparitions. Four days later, when, with great ceremony, the statue was inaugurated in the grotto at Massabielle, the talented sculptor himself felt a pang of artistic disappointment diminish his public triumph – the white marble statue, seeming perfect in his eyes when viewed in his studio or in the presbytery at Lourdes, once installed in the dark niche high up on the cliff face of rocky Massabielle was, he lamented, lit up by an unforeseen effect of light and shade that caused 'a complete change in expression'.

Neither Bernadette nor Dean Peyramale were present at the inauguration. He had decided that Bernadette should be protected from what would have been a tremendous display of veneration by the crowds. His own absence was caused by a sudden bout of illness so severe that his medical brother came from Momères to take care of him. He found the priest in an impecunious state. Far from gaining any financial benefit from the developments in Lourdes, the doctor reported that the charitable Parish Priest was spending any money he could spare on poor parishioners of his – 'there are rents of 35 poor people to pay at the end of the month to prevent evictions, and his whole fortune is 45 centimes.'

As Bernadette advanced in age and literacy, the nuns at the hospice put her in charge of lessons for some of the younger children with whom she loved to play and dance as she used to do with her own siblings and friends. Later, they introduced her to the other work of the hospice, caring for sick people. Perhaps to test or humiliate her, she was given some very unpleasant cases to deal with, like an old drunken woman who had fallen into a fire. Her response was so cheerful and dedicated that the nuns themselves must have been privately edified. This work led her to renew her hopes of becoming a nun herself. She was, in fact, being sought after by several religious orders, even to the extent of being invited to visit and try on the habit. Other orders, on the other hand, were dubious about the unwelcome effects that might arise if it became known that the visionary of Lourdes was now a nun in one of their convents. Bernadette was also the recipient of an indirect but formal and sincere offer of marriage! This came from a young medical student in Nantes who wrote, not to Bernadette, but to Bishop Laurence, from whom he received a rejection as blunt as she herself would certainly have given him.

When Bishop Forcade of Nevers, where the mother-house of the order was situated, came to Lourdes in 1863, he had a long and informal chat with Bernadette about her wish to become a nun and the obstacles to her vocation which she herself considered insurmountable. From her childhood she had been told by everyone that she was both unhealthy, uneducated and 'good for nothing'. She was now literate, but she still believed that no order would accept a poor, sickly and untalented girl. The kindly Bishop Forcade encouraged her to think otherwise, and promised that if she truly felt she had a vocation, he would see to it that nothing else need worry her.

A year later, on 4 April, the very day of the inauguration of the statue at the grotto, Bernadette attended Mass in the hospice as usual. After Mass she sought out the new Superior, Sister

Alexandrine Roques, and told her that she had now decided to become a nun, and wished to apply for permission to enter Sister Alexandrine's own order, the Sisters of Charity of Nevers, in whose care she had been living at the hospice. She had seen their work and life at first hand, of course, but later she said that one of the reasons why she chose that order was that, unlike some others, they had never tried to influence her decision.

When that decision was made known to the superiors of the order in Nevers, the Superior-General, Mother Joséphine Imbert, was not at first in favour of accepting Bernadette as a postulant because of the attention she would attract. It is recorded, however, that the Mistress of Novices, Mother Marie Thérèse Vauzou, was enthusiastic. She told her novices: 'It will be one of the great good fortunes of my life to see the eyes that have seen the Holy Virgin.' Strange to relate, when she eventually did have Bernadette, first as one of her novices and then as a colleague in the convent, the character and personality of the peasant girl from Lourdes seem to have disappointed her expectations of what a heaven-favoured visionary should be. She did not conceal her feelings, even to the extent of sometimes hinting to other nuns her doubts about the likelihood of the Mother of God deigning to appear to a simple, uneducated girl rather than to someone like a devout nun who would be more suited to such a privilege.

Bernadette was allowed to begin her postulancy at the order's convent in Lourdes in February 1865, and she was due to begin life as a novice in the mother-house at Nevers in April of the following year. Her departure was delayed at the request of Bishop Laurence who wished to have her present at another ceremony at the grotto. This was the inauguration in May of the crypt, the substructure of what would be the chapel requested in the apparitions. The bishop's request could not be countermanded by Dean Peyramale, ever anxious to keep Bernadette out of the public eye. However, when Bernadette took part in the first official procession to the grotto on 19 May, she was dressed in the blue and white uniform of the Children of Mary

and hidden in their ranks so that she would not be noticed. Later
that evening, she had to be ordered on two occasions to show
herself to the huge crowds turning up at the hospice, some of
whom added to her dismay by trying to touch her and calling on
her to bless their religious objects. She did not conceal her annoyance from the nuns: 'You show me off as if I were a freak!'
she remonstrated, 'You parade me like a prize ox!'

She was also to suffer more from the commercial photogra-
phers. One of them, Billard-Perrin, who had taken photos earlier,
came to the hospice and photographed Bernadette twice with
the community. In one photo, she wears her peasant dress and
stands behind three seated nuns and hemmed in by four others,
in the other, with the same group, she is dressed in the habit of
the order, although not yet even a novice, and seated in the centre of the front row, holding a rosary beads. Who could blame
those good nuns at Lourdes if they were secretly anxious to be
remembered as Bernadette's first religious sisters? As we have
seen, their superior, Mother Alexandrine, had set them the example a few years earlier by posing, seated, maternally holding
the hand of Bernadette who stands beside her in peasant dress.

On 2 July, two days before her departure for Nevers, another
photographer, M Viron, got permission from the bishop to take
photos of Bernadette herself and of the families on both sides.
When he offered copies as a gift to Bernadette, she insisted on
paying for them – and later gave them away to her friends. Later
that day, Bernadette went to the grotto for a quiet farewell visit.
Her Aunt Lucile said later: 'I know what she suffered in leaving
it, but she put on a brave front.'

The next evening, 3 July, the whole family gathered at the
Lacadé mill for the farewell meal. A large crowd gathered outside to see and touch her for the last time as she left. The next
morning, Bernadette's family – her mother already very ill – and
her aunts Bernarde and Basile, went to the hospice for a last
farewell. Her brother, Bernard, six years old then, later recorded
his memories: 'All of us cried, and I did what all the others did,
not really knowing the cause of all the tears.' Aunt Basile, how-

ever, testified that Bernadette herself did not cry. She consoled them by saying, 'You know I cannot stay here forever.'

On the journey to Tarbes, where she would board a train for the first time in her life and begin the long journey to Nevers by way of Bordeaux, Bernadette was accompanied by her sister, Antoinette, Aunt Bernarde and Sister Victorine. They stood on the station platform, surrounded by a crowd who had gathered, and waved goodbye as the train carried Bernadette away forever from her family and her native Lourdes.

CHAPTER SIXTEEN

The Promise Fulfilled

The city of Nevers is almost in the centre of France, nearer to Paris than to Lourdes. Bernadette may have hoped that as soon as she entered the gates of a convent so far away from the scene of the apparitions, her heart-rending sacrifice in leaving her beloved family would be balanced by a life of prayer and service lived in seclusion from the harassment that had been increasingly her lot in her native place. Whatever the nature of the three personal secrets Our Lady entrusted to her innocent soul, secrets which, at her death, she took with her back to their heavenly source, she must often have pondered on the only promise she had been given during the apparitions, that she would be happy not in this life but in the next. The thirteen years she was to spend in the convent at Nevers were to be a fulfilment of that promise. Not only did she not escape the wearying effects of her notoriety, she was also deliberately treated as unworthy and of little use by her superiors, just as she had been by the Parish Priest and the nuns in Lourdes – all for her own spiritual good, they believed – and her health, always poor, would deteriorate to the level of excruciating physical agony. Added to these personal and physical sufferings, Bernadette would also have to undergo in her final years that extreme test of faith, known as 'the dark night of the soul' from the poems of the Spanish saint, Juan de la Cruz, when satanic clouds of doubt and despair blot out all contact between the soul and God.

Bernadette did not have long to wait to realise that, when occasion demanded, she would still have to fulfil the role of 'the visionary of Lourdes'. With two other postulants and two guardian nuns, she arrived at the convent in Nevers late on the night of Saturday 7 July 1866. At 1 pm the very next day she was standing in front of a gathering in the big hall of the novitiate. She had been ordered to tell the story of the apparitions to an audience comprising not only the community of nuns, novices and postulants, but also the nuns from the order's two other convents in Nevers; also present were some of the superiors from convents in the Pyrenees, including Mother Alexandrine Roques, superior of the hospice in Lourdes. Bernadette was also ordered to wear, for the last time, the peasant clothes and the white hood in which she was now to be seen in the photos being sold all over France.

Her initiation into the humiliations that were to protect her from pride was also immediate. She was introduced to the audience of over 300 by the Mistress of Novices, Mother Marie-Thérese Vauzou, the same nun who, when the matter of Bernadette's acceptance was in the balance, had enthused to her novices, 'It will be one of the great good fortunes of my life to see the eyes that have seen the Holy Virgin.' Now that the owner of those privileged eyes was standing within arm's reach of her, she introduced her to the audience in what were later described by those who heard her as 'quite unflattering terms'.

Facing that hushed and expectant audience on her first day in the convent at Nevers, Bernadette began to speak hesitantly, and in the native *patois* in which she had told her story so often already; but as a result of an order from one of the superiors beside her, she changed to the acquired French in which she was less fluent and spontaneous. She endured further humiliation when she was describing the day on which she discovered the 'fountain' and tried three times to drink the muddy water. It was the superior from Lourdes who interjected, for the benefit of the audience, 'You can see from that how little mortified she was.' Not to be outdone, Mother Vauzou, mistress of novices, added to the rebuke, 'You were not mortified, Bernadette.' As in the case of the theologian's question about whether the Blessed Virgin wore a halo, poor Bernadette may not have known the religious meaning of the word mortification – the dictionary definition is: 'the disciplining of one's body and appetites by self-denial and austerity' – but she was quite familiar in practice with another definition of the word: 'to cause to experience shame or humiliation'. She had already been through that mill, as she might have said herself, since the day of the very first apparition. Nor was she, as many of the other forty-two postulants in her audience that day probably were, a refined teenage girl from a protected middle or upper class background. She had faced and stood up to interrogation and abuse from police and priest, from nuns and intellectual atheists and members of the general public. However, she had not yet been put through the novice's spiritual training in meek acceptance of all kinds of correction, with the result that her peasant common sense flashed out a retort which must have mortified the two superiors and perhaps given cause for secret delight to some nuns in the audience. 'Well,' said Bernadette, 'the water was very dirty!'

Three weeks later, at a ceremony presided over by Bishop Fourcade of Nevers – the kindly man who had encouraged Bernadette when he met her two years earlier in Lourdes – the postulants became novices and were given their new name in religion. Bernadette was allowed to keep her own name, linked to that of the Blessed Lady of the apparitions. Henceforth she was to be known as Sister Marie-Bernard. However, this progress in conventual status was the occasion of another sacrifice and humiliation. The custom then was that the new novices were sent to houses of the order all over France to continue their spiritual formation while also being trained in the various works of the order. To her great disappointment, Bernadette was told that she was to remain at the mother-house in Nevers. The reasons were obvious, but no consolation to Bernadette who had hoped to be treated like the others.

Perhaps it was just as well that the superiors had decided on this protective policy. A few weeks later, in August 1866, Bernadette found herself in the infirmary, afflicted with the first breakdown in her health. She could hardly eat and suffered attacks of asthma; but, as was to be the case until her final illness, her acceptance of all such suffering was simple and total: 'The good God sent this to me,' she said, 'and I must accept it.' Another candid remark of hers, referring to the professional care and religious love with which she was being treated, was a throwback to the life she had lived in Lourdes: 'The poor are not treated like this.' Her only concern was for the nun or novice assigned to watch the patients during the night; she would urge them to rest or sleep in a nearby armchair. 'I'll call you if I need you,' she told them. When she had any relief during the day from the bouts of choking, she tried to cheer up the other patients with songs in her native dialect.

On 25 October her condition deteriorated, she was vomiting blood, and the doctor declared that she would not last the night. As had happened at the hospice, she was given the Last Anointing by the chaplain. Now, however, it was decided that she should be allowed to make her religious profession as a nun because she was on the point of death. This required a dispensation from the bishop. He hurried to the convent and found her so weak that she could not say the formula of profession. The bishop said the words for her and only required her to utter Amen. Later, he was to relate that just after he left the room the dying nun recovered her voice, smiled at the Superior-General who was at her bedside with others, and said, 'You have had me make my profession because you thought I was going to die tonight. Well, I will not die tonight.' According to Bishop Forcade's account, the Superior reacted furiously and threatened to return Bernadette to the status of novice as a punishment for causing such a furore with her false alarm; but this did not happen and Bernadette was allowed to keep her professed status and the special crucifix which was its symbol.

A great personal sorrow was to conclude this initial half-year of Bernadette's life in the convent. On 8 December 1866, her mother, Louise, died. That date is the Feast of the Immaculate Conception, a significant spiritual consolation for Bernadette that did not lessen her heartbreak. It was only a few months since she had said goodbye to her family and she had suffered homesickness to the extent of shedding tears every night for some time. Louise Casterot-Soubirous was only 41 years old, but she was worn out by a life of grinding poverty, unremitting toil, and nine childbirths. Only four of her children were alive.

Recurring bouts of illness, of increasing severity, caused Bernadette to be confined to the infirmary on many more occasions until the end of her life. There were two other sources of suffering for her. The superiors had promised her that her first narration of the visions to the assembly of nuns and novices would be the last; but they could not refuse audiences to bishops, to high-ranking ecclesiastics from Rome itself, to benefactors of the order, or to people like the author, Henri Lasserre, who had been requested by the Bishop of Tarbes to write a full scholarly account of the apparitions. The third source of trial for Bernadette was the attitude adopted towards her by the mistress of novices, Mother Marie-Thérese Vauzou. As soon as Bernadette returned to the novitiate after having spent three months in the infirmary because of that first bout of serious illness, Mother Vauzou told her directly, according to the later testimony of some of Bernadette's companions, 'Now, Sister Marie-Bernard, we are going to get into the time of your testing; we are going to come down on you.' Bernadette replied, with a smile, 'Oh, Mother, I hope you will do it gently!' As time went on, Mother Vauzou began to express doubts about the apparitions at Lourdes, even to the extent of mentioning that some bishops did not believe in them. Yet, she was so highly regarded as a nun that she was elected Superior-General of the Order, a post she held from 1881 (two years after Bernadette's death) to 1899. When her successor told her about the cause for the beatification of Bernadette, she said, 'Wait until after I am dead.' Strange to say, when the day of her death came, her last prayer was: 'Our Lady of Lourdes, protect me in my death agony.' Once, during her own last illness, when Bernadette was speaking of what she called her two jobs on earth, prayer and sacrifice, she said that in heaven she would continue the job of prayer; she must surely have put in a word for that good nun who seems sometimes to have doubted the truth of her story.

Although Bernadette had been professed as a nun when it was thought that she was at the point of death early in her novitiate, she took part with forty-three other novices in the formal ceremony of profession, presided over by Bishop Forcade, on 30 October 1867. Later that day, another ceremony took place. In the presence of the community, each of the newly-professed nuns was called in turn to be presented by Bishop Forcade with a crucifix, the book containing the constitutions of the Order, and the letter of obedience directing her to some house of the Order. For this ceremony, the Mother-General had consulted with the bishop about the problem of what to do with Sister Marie-Bernard – they knew that she could not be sent to any outside convent. However, to keep a newly-professed nun at the mother-house of the Order would be most unusual, and to do so with Bernadette might be interpreted as favouring her because of her status as the visionary. Sister Marie-Bernard had to endure another humiliation because of that status. The bishop called each new nun in turn, leaving Sister Marie-Bernard until last.

'And now, what about Sister Marie-Bernard?' he said to the Mother-General. She replied that Sister Marie-Bernard could not be sent anywhere – because she was good for nothing. The bishop called her name and when she approached, he gave her no letter but called out her assignment in a loud voice.

'Sister Marie-Bernard – nowhere!'

But then he spoke kindly to her. 'Is it true that you are good for nothing?'

'Yes, it's true,' she replied humbly, with her usual candour. But, true to form, she reminded him of their previous encounter. 'I told you that in Lourdes when you said I might enter this order, and you told me it would not matter.' Of course, the good bishop had not forgotten.

'Well then, my poor child,' he said gently, 'I wonder what are we going to do with you?'

Mother Josephine intervened with the pre-arranged suggestion. 'If you agree, Your Excellency, out of charity we could keep her here in the mother-house and give her some sort of work in the infirmary, even if it be only to clean up and help with meals for the sick sisters. Since she herself is always ill, it would be something she would understand.'

The bishop asked Bernadette if she would be willing to accept this assignment.

'I will try,' she said honestly.

Then Bishop Forcade spoke from his heart. 'Sister Marie-Bernarde, I give you the job of prayer.' He knew her real worth.

CHAPTER SEVENTEEN

The Final Agony

Bernadette accepted both jobs, the concocted one as helper to
Sister Marthe, the infirmarian, and the spiritual task of prayer
given her by the bishop, with her usual cheerfulness and resig-
nation to God's will. Her increase in holiness to the stage where
she would later be declared a saint was not marked by any os-
tentation, but was of benefit to all around her in her charity and
dedication. As the years went on, while her superiors never re-
lented in their official care to protect her from pride, they made
good use of her true piety and cheerful personality for the benefit of other young nuns and novices who might have been inhib-
ited in their dealings with official counsellors. Even when she
was confined to bed herself, novices were sent to help in the infirmary so that they could learn both from Sister Marie-
Bernard's patience in suffering and from her simple but deep
spiritual insights.

Her experience as a helper with the sick in the hospice at
Lourdes had prepared Bernadette for her new job as helper in
the infirmary at the mother-house; but the menial jobs she was
given at first did not require any particular skill. During the
novitiate, she had been assigned to cleaning the toilets, and most
of the work she now undertook was of the same kind. But while
her cheerfulness and humour were like a tonic to the patients,
she was also well able to exert control and authority when necessary. The nuns and novices who were her patients soon
learned that Sister Marie-Bernard, willing to exert herself to the
utmost for their welfare, would put up with no nonsense.
Meanwhile, Sister Marthe, the infirmarian, who was herself unwell, noticing how eager and apt her new assistant was, began to

inculcate her into a higher level of work, teaching her the various treatments and medical prescriptions that were part of the daily routine. That training would prove to be providential.

In her second year as assistant infirmarian, Bernadette suffered another setback in health. She spent Easter as a patient in the infirmary, and was confined there a second time in the Autumn, 'spitting up whole basins of blood' as the infirmarian recorded. She also confided to the Superior-General, 'The doctor says she could die in a fit of spitting blood.' As on previous occasions, however, Bernadette showed remarkable resilience. No sooner was she on her feet again than she was subjected to a new bout of torment from another source. Two conflicting authors of the history of the apparitions each got permission from the bishop to visit the visionary herself. This they did in turn, questioning her at length and in minute detail, and recording her answers. Apart from the physical and mental strain involved, Bernadette suffered great distress from the fact that the apparitions were now becoming a cause of scholarly dispute and that she herself was increasingly unable to recall the details or the exact chronology of the events that had changed her life.

In April 1870, both Sister Marthe and Sister Marie-Bernarde, the two infirmarians, were confined to bed at the same time. Once again, some observers thought that Bernadette was so ill that she was at death's door; but she herself reassured one of them, 'Tell Mother Superior not to worry herself, because I will not die today.'

That same year, 1870, saw the invasion of France by the Prussian-led coalition of German states. The defeat of the French at Sedan led to the deposition of the emperor, Napoleon III, and the formation of the Third Republic. Paris was besieged by the Prussians, and in November they advanced towards Nevers. In a letter to her father, Bernadette wrote: 'They say that the enemy is approaching Nevers. I could do without seeing the Prussians, but I am not afraid of them. God is everywhere, even among the Prussians … I fear only bad Catholics.'

That was the last letter François Soubirous received from his beloved daughter. He died on 4 March, the anniversary of the last apparition in the series of fifteen resulting from the courteous request of Our Lady to the young Bernadette. Some days later, another nun found Sister Marie-Bernarde leaning against the chimney in tears, the letter bearing the sad news in her hand.

Another death had a different kind of impact on Bernadette's life. Sister Marthe's health had deteriorated even more and she was sent away for a rest. Bernadette took over as infirmarian and proved herself totally competent. She had been a keen student under Sister Marthe's guidance and had assiduously written out all the details of measurements and other factors involved in the various treatments. Sister Marthe returned for a while but became ill again towards the end of 1870. She died in November 1872. Bernadette had been in full charge of the infirmary during the enforced absences of Sister Marthe; now, she was allowed to continue in that position but without the official title of infirmarian. Lack of the title did not bother her – she was working for God, not for any plaudits, titles or other rewards. However, God saw fit to let it be known to the world at large that the peasant girl who had seen the apparitions at Lourdes was gifted with intelligence and natural talents which she had developed by dedicated application.

In spite of all that Louis Veuillot, editor of *L'Univers*, or anyone else might say in support of the events at Lourdes and of the integrity of Bernadette, there would always be anti-Catholic journalists and writers – the novelist, Emile Zola, a later prominent example – who decried the alleged apparitions and belittled the visionary herself. In September 1872, one Dr Voisin, who was attached to an asylum for aged and mentally ill women in Paris, published the following verdict: 'The miracle of Lourdes was sanctioned on the testimony of a child suffering from hallucinations who is now shut away in the convent of the Ursulines of Nevers' – one hopes he did not confuse his patients as he confused the religious orders of nuns.

In a reply to this nonsense, the distinguished medical man who was official physician to the mother-house of the Sisters of

Charity at Nevers, Dr Robert Saint-Cyr – he was also the president of the Medical Association – published the following verdict on the status and work of Sister Marie-Bernarde: 'She is an infirmarian who fulfils her task to perfection. Small and puny, she is 27 years old. She has a calm and gentle nature. She takes care of her sick patients with a great deal of intelligence, leaving out nothing in the prescriptions ordered. She also exercises great authority and has my full confidence.'

It is likely that this glowing professional encomium was read with satisfaction by the nuns both in Paris and Nevers, but it was probably kept from the sickly but dedicated young woman who was its subject. Unfortunately, Bernadette's own health suffered serious relapses again during the following year In June, 1873, she received the Anointing of the Sick for the third time, recovered again, and joked: 'They don't want me up there just yet!' In October of that year, her superiors decided it was time to relieve her of the onerous duties of infirmarian. They did it by demoting her to her former position as assistant, this time to Sister Gabriel de Vigouroux, a nun two years younger than Sister Marie-Bernarde. Apparently, the new infirmarian did not take kindly to any helpful suggestions offered by the humble nun she replaced, which might explain the resolution formed by Bernadette at the end of her retreat in July 1875 'to strive to become indifferent.'

On relieving her of the post of infirmarian, her superiors added the lighter duties of assistant sacristan to those of assistant infirmarian. However, Bernadette continued to undertake some of the more unpleasant tasks in the infirmary. A nun who testified to this at the canonisation process, as well as to many other manifestations of the heroic sanctity of Sister Marie-Bernarde, was none other than Julie Garros, who as a ten-year-old child had been assigned to help the sixteen-year-old Bernadette Soubirous in her studies when she was taken in as a boarder at the hospice in Lourdes. Their roles were reversed when Julie arrived at the convent in Nevers as a novice and was assigned to learn how to care for the sick under the direction of

Sister Marie-Bernarde. They surely must have reminisced about those tempting strawberries! Julie was an important witness in the canonisation process, revealing how Bernadette chided her into overcoming her natural fastidiousness in dealing with unpleasant physical afflictions – 'A fine Sister of Charity you'll make!' – but also to persevere in her vocation when she was feeling discouraged. The quality of Bernadette's own vocation was obvious, both in her care of the sick and in the profound spirituality of the things she said; but, worldly wise from her peasant environment and from her early experience with the sick in the Lourdes hospice, she also had some practical advice for the younger nun when she was being sent out as an infirmarian to some hospice: 'Whenever you're alone in a room with men, make sure the door is open.'

In June 1876 a delegation from Nevers, led by Bishop Ladoue – Bernadette's benevolent counsellor, Bishop Forcade, had been appointed Archbishop of Aix – was setting out for Lourdes to be present at the consecration of the new basilica. The bishop asked Bernadette if she would like to go with them. She refused, as she always did such offers. Confidentially, however, she told others that if she could 'go to the grotto when nobody was there and pray for a few moments, then I would gladly go'. When someone showed her photos of the grotto, now altered to make the approaches and surrounding area safer for the many pilgrims, Bernadette exclaimed sadly: 'Oh, my poor grotto! I would not recognise it any more.' She gave Bishop Ladoue a letter for her old friend, Dean Peyramale. The Parish Priest of Lourdes was feeling depressed by developments. He had been removed from control of affairs there, and even his parish church was now almost empty. He replied kindly to Bernadette's message: 'Tell her that she is still my child and that I give her my blessing.' He died on 8 September in the following year, 1877. It was the Feast of the Birth of Our Lady. The nun who conveyed the sad news to Bernadette while she was at prayer saw her weep for the kind but gruff priest to whom she had conveyed Our Lady's request for a chapel and a procession. Another item of news from

Lourdes caused grief of a different kind; it was when Bernadette learned that her sister, Toinette, and her brother, Pierre, were both now fully involved in the ever-increasing commercial trade that was an inevitable result of the apparitions seen by their sister. That understandable involvement by the Soubirous family continues today, as visitors to the Maison Paternelle de Ste Bernadette, the old dungeon home of the saint, are made aware by a notice concerning the adjoining shop.

Bishop Ladoue, who had invited Bernadette to go with him to Lourdes in June 1876, was back with another request in December. He was about to go to Rome, and he decided to bring a letter from Bernadette to Pope Pius IX in which she would ask for a papal blessing. Bernadette had little choice but to comply, although she was in bed again and suffering now from an extra affliction in the form of a very painful tumour on one of her knees. She wrote the letter in bed, using a small stool placed across her knees. However, the plain style of the peasant girl from Lourdes did not satisfy the bishop or the nuns. The letter had to be re-written, with suggested changes and additions. It was then copied out by a nun on the official stationery of the Order. Then Bernadette was told to copy this in her best handwriting; inevitably, she became confused and even made some spelling mistakes. She had to write it all out again, no matter what pain or fatigue it might cause.

What Pope Pius IX thought of the letter is not known, but the papal blessing duly came back from Rome. Bishop Ladoue was lucky he did not hear what Sister Marie-Bernarde thought of him. 'He's small and cold,' she told another nun, 'he won't last long.' He died six months later. When her own death seemed imminent yet again, she said to one of the nuns detailed to watch over her at night, 'Don't trouble yourself so often, get some rest. They think I'm going to die, but I still have more than six months to go.' Perhaps the time of her death was one of the personal secrets confided to her by Our Blessed Lady.

As we have seen, the nuns were unable to refuse the requests of eminent visitors like bishops who wished to speak with

Bernadette, but they refused the request of the Jesuit historian, Fr Cros, when he came to the convent in August 1878, asking to interview her in connection with the official history of the apparitions which he had been asked to write. An early and firm believer in the apparitions, he had met Bernadette twice while she lived at the hospice in Lourdes with the intention of writing his book then; however, his superiors ordered him to put this aside and continue with the biography of St John Berchmans SJ, on which he had been working. Now at last he was working on the Lourdes book. Unfortunately, many people, including Bernadette's parents and Dean Peyramale, were dead; but he had already interviewed over two hundred witnesses, including Bernadette's sister, Toinette, and Jeanne Abadie, their companion on the fateful 11 February 1858.

There were already, as has been seen, acrimonious disputes between various authors concerning the events at Lourdes, and the nuns, like Bernadette herself, had no wish to be involved. Eventually, Fr Cros enlisted the aid of the Archbishop of Reims who was going to Rome. He brought back a letter from the new Pope, Leo XIII, giving his approval of the project and urging people to give testimony. The nuns at Nevers complied with this request, but without allowing Fr Cros direct access to Sister Marie-Bernarde. They disliked what they considered his prying scholarly methods. They allowed Fr Sempé, a modest and discreet priest who was a curate in Lourdes and who had impressed them during an earlier dispute, to present Bernadette with the list of fifty questions the Jesuit historian had prepared.

To many of these questions, the ailing Bernadette could only reply, 'I don't remember.' Her illness and her failing memory for details of the events left her confused. She even spoke once as if all the words of Our Lady had been conveyed to her at one apparition. Fr Cros was not satisfied. He sent back another list of queries. The nuns would have liked to protect Bernadette, but the Jesuit scholar was backed by a papal letter. Finally, they themselves had to present her with more questions from Fr Cros on three different occasions, the final one only a month before she died. In a conversation with one of her superiors just a week before she died, those interrogations and disputes were still troubling her mind. 'As for me,' she said, 'I want no disputes. I certainly advised my relatives to stay out of it.' She added: 'I have told the events. Let people abide by what I said the first time. I may have forgotten some things and so may other people.'

Some idea of the excruciating physical agony endured by Bernadette in the final months of her life can be gained from an account by the convent infirmarian found in the notes of the meticulous Fr Cros: 'Ankylosis of the knee. Terrible pain: a huge knee, impaired leg, which one hardly knew how to move. Sometimes it took an hour to change her position. Her facial expression changed greatly: she became like a corpse. She, who was very energetic in her desire for suffering, was completely vanquished by the pain. Even while sleeping, the least movement of the leg drew a cry of anguish from her ... and these cries prevented her companions in the infirmary from sleeping. She passed whole nights without sleep. In her pain and suffering she shrunk down almost to nothing.'

To this can be added the words of Fr Febvre, her last confessor, who visited her frequently up to the time of her death: 'Chronic asthma, chest pains, accompanied by spitting of blood that went on for two years. An aneurism, gastralgia, and a tumour of the knee ... Finally, during the last few years she suffered from bone decay, so that her poor body was the vessel of all kinds of pain and suffering. Meanwhile abscesses formed in her ears, inflicting partial deafness on her. This was very painful for her and ceased only a short time before her death.' A sentence in the infirmarian's testimony sums it all up: 'Her poor body was just one big sore.' Bernadette never spoke about miracles and never asked anyone to pray that she might be cured. When she heard that people in Lourdes were doing a special novena to ask Our Lady's intercession for her, her response was that they be requested not to do so.

Her mind going back to her childhood in the Boly mill, the

dying Sister Marie-Bernarde said one day to the nun attending her: 'I have been ground in the mill like a grain of wheat. I would never have thought that one must suffer so much to die.' Another nun recorded what might seem a bizarre incident to the modern reader: only two weeks before she died, Bernadette's hair was cut for the last time as it had been periodically; apparently it was used to raise money for the ransom of slaves in Africa. In all the intensity of her pain, Bernadette herself explained it simply: 'It's to buy a black woman.'

From Fr Febvre also we get some intimation of the other agony with which the dying Bernadette was afflicted, the spiritual agony of a satanic mist that clouded over her faith and hope. He was the priest who supported her during this crisis of the soul. One of the theological questions put to her during an interrogation years earlier was to the effect that if Our Lady had promised to make her happy in heaven, she was sure of salvation and need not worry about how she lived. Bernadette had countered that by saying that the promise meant she would be saved if she lived a good life of prayer and penance as Our Lady had wished. Now one of the temptations to despair tormenting her soul was the thought that she had not done enough to thank God for the great favours she had received. A few days before her death, her confessor heard her say several times, 'Get away from me, Satan!' He says: 'She told me that the devil had tried to frighten her, but that she had invoked the holy name of Jesus and the whole thing had disappeared.' Before that spiritual agony began, she had told Fr Febvre that she was praying to St Joseph for 'the grace of a happy death' (he is officially the patron of that final grace). Her prayer was answered. Fr Febvre administered the Sacrament of the Sick – it was the fourth time since the night in the hospice at Lourdes in 1868 when the doctor predicted that Bernadette 'would not last the night'. Bernadette died on 16 April 1879. One of her last utterances linked the saintly, humble nun with the poor, illiterate girl who had instinctively reached for her beads when she saw that first apparition in the grotto at Massabielle: 'Holy Mary, Mother of God, pray for me, poor sinner.'

Although she had hoped to hide herself away in the convent at Nevers, Bernadette's name and fame were now worldwide. As soon as news of her death went beyond the convent, crowds came flocking to see her in her coffin. In conjunction with the increase of pilgimages to Lourdes and the evidence of miracles, the cause for canonisation of Bernadette proceeded to gain momentum. In September 1909, the Bishop of Nevers gave permission for the exhumation of her body. It was found to be incorrupt, as it was again on the occasion of a second exhumation in connection with the process of canonisation. Today, the saint's incorrupt body, resting in a casket of bronze and crystal at the convent in Nevers, is an object of veneration by the thousands of pilgrims who come to pray there.

Bernadette was beatified in 1925 by Pope Pius XI, and canonised by him in 1933 on 8 December, the Feast of the Immaculate Conception of the Blessed Virgin Mary.